Dec. '90

See p 46

The Bright Sparks
of Wireless

by George Jessop G6JP

Radio Society of Great Britain

Published by the Radio Society of Great Britain, Cranborne Road, Potters bar, Herts. EN6 3JE

ISBN 0 900612 95 9

Cover Design and Typography by S. Clark, Radio Society of Great Britain.
Printed in Great Britain by The Bath Press, Lower Bristol Road, Bath. BA2 3BL.

Contents

This book is dedicated to the Radio
Amateur Old Timers Association, many
of whose members contributed to the
early advancement of radio
communication and the Society's
progress over many years.

A. A. Campbell-Swinton, FRS., M.Inst.CE., MIEE., 2HK. Founder President of the Radio Society of Great Britain 1913 – 1920.

A collection of early small Triode valves.

Chapter 1

In the Beginning...

The organisation which was ultimately to become the Radio Society of Great Britain was founded in 1913 - but the story of early radio (or, if you prefer, 'wireless') really starts some years earlier. The book 'BBC Engineering 1922-1972' by Edward Pawley, dealing with the history of BBC engineering sums it up rather well and introduces us to some names which will shortly become familiar :

> The possibility of conveying messages over a distance without wires emerged from a series of experiments starting with the discoveries of Professor D. E. Hughes and Heinrich Hertz. In 1879 Hughes produced electric sparks in his house at 40 Langham Street, London – near where Broadcasting House now stands – and detected them at distances up to 450 metres whilst walking up and down Great Portland Street by means of a microphonic contact and a telephone earpiece. The pundits of that time refused to accept that the effect was produced by 'aerial electric waves' and so Hughes' discovery remained unpublished until after Hertz had conclusively proved, in 1887, that electromagnetic waves at frequencies below those of light could be detected at a distance. He used an induction coil to produce sparks across a gap between two metal balls. At the receiving end, a few metres away, sparks appeared across a gap introduced into a metal loop. Hertz thus verified the existence of electromagnetic waves, of which James Clerk Maxwell had postulated the existence by mathematical reasoning in 1862. Hertz explained their properties and the differences between light and electricity in a lecture at Heidelberg in September 1889. He himself said that his discovery could not be used for a practical purpose. At a meeting of the British Association in 1894 Sir Oliver Lodge demonstrated actual radiotelegraphy over a distance of 55 metres, using Hertz's oscillator in conjunction with a receiver containing a Branley coherer. Because of his academic duties, Lodge failed to follow up this experiment and, like Hertz, he apparently thought that there was no future for radio communications because range would be limited to a few hundred metres. Fortunately, later experimenters were not deterred by these gloomy prognostications.

In 1896 the eminent electrical engineer A A Campbell-Swinton wrote a letter of introduction to the Engineer in Chief of the General Post Office (GPO) on behalf of a young Italian inventor by the name of Guglielmo Marconi.

Both men are prominent in our story. Campbell-Swinton's name is not as familiar today as Marconi's but his technical insight may be gauged from his description on paper, in 1907-11, of the principles of a workable television system.

Coming back to the turn of the century, 'Wireless Telegraphy' was clearly going to become a valuable means of communication and therefore a governmental asset. At the end of the Victorian age 'regulated' meant 'very strictly regulated', and the Wireless Telegraphy Act 1904 – which introduced the concept of a licence for the establishment of a wireless telegraph station – was suitably draconian. Section 2(1) of the Act made grudging reference to those wanting licences for experimental purposes. They were to be granted '.... subject to such special terms, conditions and restrictions as the Postmaster-General shall think proper ....', although no fee was chargeable.

Despite the implied restrictions, the fascination of wireless held the interest of various dedicated 'experi-

A. A. CAMPBELL SWINTON.
ELECTRICAL ENGINEER.

Telegraphic Address.
"DUNAMIS, LONDON."

TELEPHONE Nº3/55.

66, Victoria Street,
London, S.W.

March 30 th. 1896.

Dear Mr Preece,

I am taking the liberty of sending to you with this note a young Italian of the name of Marconi, who has come over to this country with the idea of getting taken up a new system of telegraphy without wires, at which he has been working. It appears to be based upon the use of Hertzian waves, and Oliver Lodge's coherer, but from what he tells me he appears to have got considerably beyond what I believe other people have done in this line.

It has occurred to me that you might possibly be kind enough to see him and hear what he has to say and I also think that what he

has done will very likely be of interest to you.

Hoping that I am not troubling you too much.

Believe me,

Yours very truly,

A. A. C. Swinton

W. H. Preece Esq. C.B.

Guglielmo Marconi
101 Hereford Rd
Bayswater   Bologna

The historic letter in which Alan A. Campbell-Swinton introduced Guglielmo Marconi to W. H. Preece, Engineer in Chief of the British Post Office, is of particular interest to members of the Society, because it was written by the man who some years later became the founder president of the Wireless Society of London.

menters'. Some were professional engineers in various disciplines, others were wholly self-taught. Before looking at the consequences in detail, however, it is interesting to recall some basic facts about life at the beginning of the twentieth century, when the early wireless experimenters were becoming active. Electricity itself was hardly a household word, and indeed the average home did not have a domestic electricity supply. Lighting was by means of gas or oil lamps, London's Underground railways were still using steam locomotives and most traffic in the streets was horse-drawn. When electricity supplies were available, they varied widely both in form and voltage; they could be DC or AC and anywhere between 100 and 250V. In the case of an AC supply the frequency could be anything between 25 and 100 Hz depending on the supplier. This meant that power supplies for wireless apparatus

were a major problem, and it is not surprising that in the early days power levels were generally quite low. Operating voltages were most often obtained from batteries charged from a dynamo driven by gas engine or water-wheel.

Information on wireless equipment appeared in the 'Marconigraph' magazine (later to become 'Wireless World'), the 'Model Engineer' and similar magazines. However, suppliers of equipment were few and far between. The celebrated emporium of A W Gamage in High Holborn, London, was very popular; others such as H W Sullivan offered a range of components but, in relation to the average weekly wage at that time, they were very expensive. Happily, many of the early experimenters had considerable experience of model-making and were used to making for themselves items which could not be otherwise obtained.

LETTERS TO THE EDITOR.

[*The Editor does not hold himself responsible for opinions expressed by his correspondents. Neither can he undertake to return, or to correspond with the writers of, rejected manuscripts intended for this or any other part of* NATURE. *No notice is taken of anonymous communications.*]

Distant Electric Vision.

REFERRING to Mr. Shelford Bidwell's illuminating communication on this subject published in NATURE of June 4, may I point out that though, as stated by Mr. Bidwell, it is wildly impracticable to effect even 160,000 synchronised operations per second by ordinary mechanical means, this part of the problem of obtaining distant electric vision can probably be solved by the employment of two beams of kathode rays (one at the transmitting and one at the receiving station) synchronously deflected by the varying fields of two electromagnets placed at right angles to one another and energised by two alternating electric currents of widely different frequencies, so that the moving extremities of the two beams are caused to sweep synchronously over the whole of the required surfaces within the one-tenth of a second necessary to take advantage of visual persistence.

Indeed, so far as the receiving apparatus is concerned, the moving kathode beam has only to be arranged to impinge on a sufficiently sensitive fluorescent screen, and given suitable variations in its intensity, to obtain the desired result.

The real difficulties lie in devising an efficient transmitter which, under the influence of light and shade, shall sufficiently vary the transmitted electric current so as to produce the necessary alterations in the intensity of the kathode beam of the receiver, and further in making this transmitter sufficiently rapid in its action to respond to the 160,000 variations per second that are necessary as a minimum.

Possibly no photoelectric phenomenon at present known will provide what is required in this respect, but should something suitable be discovered, distant electric vision will, I think, come within the region of possibility.

A. A. CAMPBELL SWINTON.

66 Victoria Street, London, S.W., June 12.

From 'Nature', issue of 18 June 1908

Campbell-Swinton's proposal for television in 1908!

[4 EDW. 7.] *Wireless Telegraphy Act, 1904.* [CH. **24.**]

CHAPTER 24.

An Act to provide for the regulation of Wireless Telegraphy. [15th August 1904.]

A.D. 1904.

BE it enacted by the King's most Excellent Majesty, by and with the advice and consent of the Lords Spiritual and Temporal, and Commons, in this present Parliament assembled, and by the authority of the same, as follows :—

1.—(1) A person shall not establish any wireless telegraph station, or instal or work any apparatus for wireless telegraphy, in any place or on board any British ship except under and in accordance with a licence granted in that behalf by the Postmaster-General.

Licences for wireless telegraphy.

(2) Every such licence shall be in such form and for such period as the Postmaster-General may determine, and shall contain the terms, conditions, and restrictions on and subject to which the licence is granted, and any such licence may include two or more stations, places, or ships.

(3) If any person establishes a wireless telegraph station without a licence in that behalf, or instals or works any apparatus for wireless telegraphy without a licence in that behalf, he shall be guilty of a misdemeanour, and be liable, on conviction under the Summary Jurisdiction Acts, to a penalty not exceeding ten pounds, and on conviction on indictment to a fine not exceeding one hundred pounds, or to imprisonment, with or without hard labour, for a term not exceeding twelve months, and in either case be liable to forfeit any apparatus for wireless telegraphy installed or worked without a licence, but no proceedings shall be taken against any person under this Act except by order of the Postmaster-General, the Admiralty, the Army Council, or the Board of Trade.

(4) If a justice of the peace is satisfied by information on oath that there is reasonable ground for supposing that a wireless

[*Price ½d.*] 1

The Wireless Telegraphy Act 1904.

The Early Stations

Later on you will find illustrations of a number of early stations. In respect of the equipment used they are all basically similar, varying only in details dependent on the personal choice and skill of the operator.

In essence each station consisted of a spark transmitter and a crystal detector receiver. Taking the transmitter first, this was a relatively simple item. It consisted of an induction coil for production of the high voltage for the spark across its output terminals; this was connected directly to the tuned circuit, the inductance of which was usually about 12 inches in diameter and supported on a wooden-frame former. Taps could be made to change the operating wavelength. An alternative type of inductor was the "spider-web" coil

Transmitter inductances: The helix, left, was the most frequently used in spark transmitters and right, the 'spider web' coil or 'pancake'.

The tuning capacitor (universally referred to in those days as a condenser) was either a series of Leyden jars in parallel or - more frequently - some form of variable, with either two sets of plates sliding together horizontally with glass insulation (often made from old cleaned photographic plates) or a rotary type. This took much longer to make since all the component parts had to be made by the constructor; it implied cutting the plates, obtaining the support side rods (usually standard brass studding), making or buying the necessary spacer washers and making suitable end plates.

Often the variable condenser would be built into a suitable container so that it could be oil-filled. At that period insulators were not readily available and suitable components had to be home-made; such things as small glass jam jars were successfully used. Considerable experimentation to establish the optimum material for spark gaps took place; various shapes and

materials were used, together with cooling devices close to the tip. All types of spark gap were very noisy and soon became enclosed in "mufflers"

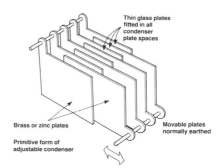

A primitive form of adjustable condenser.

As far as the receiver was concerned, assembly of this item offered a greater opportunity for personal skill and ingenuity. Unlike the transmitter, a wide tuning range was necessary for the receiver so that commercial high-power stations could be received; these carried news bulletins and also, in the case of the well-known Paris station "FL", time signals.

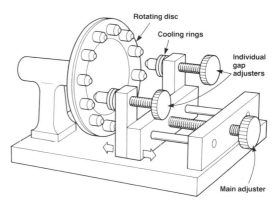

An open rotary spark gap.

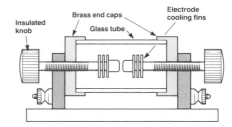

An enclosed (muffled) simple spark gap.

Typical 'tuners' consisted either of a double slider (variable tapping) inductance or a 'double circuit tuner' in which one coil slid inside another. Both had some means of varying the amount of coil in circuit.

A rotary spark gap constructed by A. E. Vick, Birmingham, WVX, 1912, later G5BL. It was used with his transmitter of 10 watts input, which had a range of six miles on 100 metres and a receiver tuning range of 100 to 200 metres.

Receiver tuning coils: The loose coupler tapped type.

Undoubtedly the most interesting portion of the receiver was the crystal detector, and a good deal of attention was paid to this component by experimenters. Since in the early days there were no valves, and hence no amplification of signals was possible, any increase in detection sensitivity which could be achieved was very beneficial. There was considerable difference of opinion; some preferred the two-crystal 'Perikon' type whilst others still clung to the earlier electrolytic detector. When the crystal detector came into use it was much favoured since it was considerably more sensitive. The two-crystal type was followed by the single crystal with a point contact, later to become known as the 'cat's whisker'. This enabled the user to find the most sensitive spot.

It was soon found necessary to devise a method of protecting the detector from damage during periods of transmission. This led to the construction of electrical or mechanical methods of separating the two crystals in 'Perikon' detectors or immersion of the point-contact type in oil. The more recently introduced 'carborundum' detector - with its potentiometer for adjustment of the bias voltage to give optimum performance - was favoured by some constructors. Various types of detector are illustrated. In passing, it is interesting to note that constructors were quite prepared to do such things as simple glass-blowing to fit a platinum wire into a glass thimble for use in the electrolytic detector shown in the diagram!

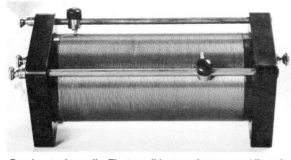

Receiver tuning coils: The two slider type, known as a 'Jigger'.

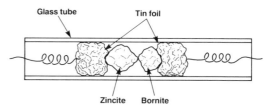

A. E. Vick's perikon detector, 1910/12. Some early perikon detectors were made as illustrated above, they were, of course, not adjustable as in the later types.

Receiver tuning coils: The loose coupler slider type.

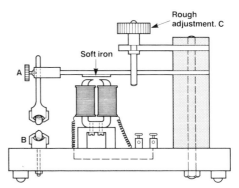

Perikon crystal detector arranged for automatic disconnection: Magnetically operated type.

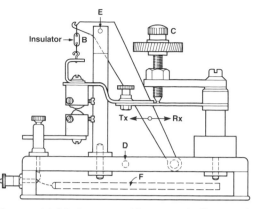

Perikon crystal detector arranged for automatic disconnection: Mechanically operated type.

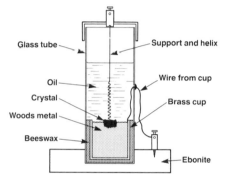

An example of an oil immersed point contact detector (E. Cathery).

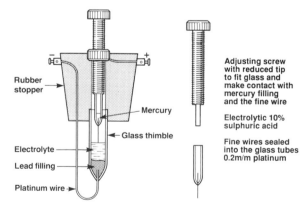

Adjusting screw with reduced tip to fit glass and make contact with mercury filling and the fine wire

Electrolytic 10% sulphuric acid

Fine wires sealed into the glass tubes 0.2m/m platinum

One design of an electrolytic detector.

The various materials used for crystal detectors - both as two-crystal combinations and as single crystal with its preferred contact metal - are as follows. With the exception of carborundum, all were operated without static bias; carborundum was usually operated with about 0.8V across the junction, provided by a dry battery and potentiometer.

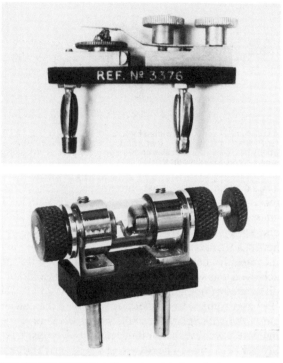

Two versions of plug-in carborundum detectors, the lower example (German) having a pointed steel contact.

Single crystal metal combinations

Carborundum - steel
Galena - brass
Galena - copper
Galena - gold
Galena - silver
Silicon - steel
Silicon - gold
Iron pyrites - gold
Iron pyrites - silver
Molybdenite - copper

Two-crystal combinations

Zincite - chalcopyrite
Zincite - tellurium
Zincite - copper pyrites
Zincite - bornite
Galena - tellurium
Galena - graphite

Of these, galena for point-contact, zincite-bornite and carborundum became the most widely used. Carborundum was adopted by the Army and was used in the Mark III trench receiver.

A Typical Early Crystal Receiver

In the early days, when component symbols had not come into use, what we would nowadays call the 'circuit diagram' was more pictorial. In the associated illustration the coils A and B are coupled together by means of one sliding inside the other. The variable condenser was made with flat zinc plates; the two sets were insulated from each other with thin glass plates and slid into and out of each other. Since glass has a dielectric constant about seven times that of air, relatively high values of capacitance could be obtained.

The potentiometer is made from some 23 feet of 'nosegay' wire, which presumably is some form of iron wire; no indication of any resistance value is shown on the drawing.

Note that the cost of materials for such a receiver was some two guineas - about £90 in 1988 currency!

The aerial used a twin wire top some 240 feet long at an average height of 30 feet. Insulators were made from small jam pots, drilled with a file fixed to a carpenter's brace!

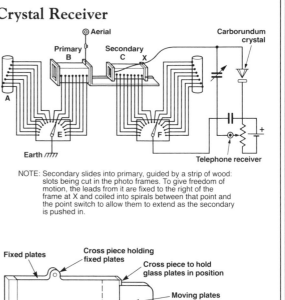

NOTE: Secondary slides into primary, guided by a strip of wood: slots being cut in the photo frames. To give freedom of motion, the leads from it are fixed to the right of the frame at X and coiled into spirals between that point and the point switch to allow them to extend as the secondary is pushed in.

Fixed plates — Cross piece holding fixed plates — Cross piece to hold glass plates in position — Moving plates — End of fixed plates — Stop to prevent pulling right out

Two simple single crystal detectors: A precision detector with brass tipped steel blade with silicon crystal, (H. W. Sullivan) pre 1914, above, and a detector with a carborundum steel blade as used in the Army mark III receiver during the 1914/18 war.

Home made headphones made by A. E. Vick, later G5BL, Porlock, Somerset, in 1910. Bobbins were wound with 50 swg dsc wire and magnet flashed across using 220v DC to magnetise. Wooden pillboxes were used for the bodies.

Three Early Stations

No.1: W K Alford, TXK (later 2DX), Kendal 1913

Power: 25W

Wavelength: 200 metres

Range: 5-7 miles

This station was established in 1912; Alford's interest in wireless began at an early age and he was one of the few stations to copy the names of survivors of the 'Titanic' disaster. His transmitter had a 10" spark; it was powered by a 35V 12A dynamo driven by a gas engine, which charged a 14-cell battery for the spark coil. The aerial was a 48 feet four-wire cage. Tuning was by means of a spider-web coil and a bank of nine Leyden jars. The receiver was a typical crystal type using 'Perikon' detectors. The most favoured crystal combinations were zincite-bornite or zincite-tellurium.

Alford arranged tests with an aircraft flying over Lake Windermere. The pilot was provided with a spark transmitter, which apparently he was rather frightened of using!

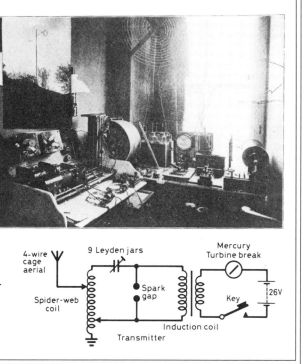

The aerial was either coupled to the main tuned circuit of the transmitter by another coil or, more often, tapped directly on the tuned circuit! This obviously meant that the aerial had to be very well insulated, as did any counterpoise used. Keying the transmitter was usually performed in the primary of the induction coil. The operating wavelength was quite varied and could be anywhere between 100 and 600 metres; however, 200 metres appears to have been the most popular choice. In general terms, aerials were as high as possible and consisted of as much wire as could be found room for. Usually the aerial proper consisted of a multi-wire top arranged either as a "flat top" or as a cage with four or six wires separated by hoops at each end, sometimes with a hoop at each end to keep the wires in place.

The first Directory of Experimental Stations (ancestor of the modern Call Book) was published by A W Gamage in July 1913 and a second edition appeared in March 1914. From this we have produced a map showing the location of stations. See the following pages for the map and histograms of range, power and wavelength.

The London Wireless Club/Wireless Society of London

Amateur experimentation in wireless communication was largely inspired by the considerable publicity given to the work done by Marconi and his associates and such disasters as the Titanic sinking. For many years wireless material was only published in the *Model Engineer*, with some other articles in other popular magazines. It was not until the *Marconigraph* appeared in April, 1911, that any magazine wholly devoted to wireless was available. After 2 years this magazine was taken over and became the *Wireless World*.

Early wireless equipment had much in common with model engineering when there was virtually no

(N.B. Only 60% of London stations shown)

A map of Great Britain and Northern Ireland showing the locations of early stations which were recorded in *A W Gamage's Directory of Experimental Stations*.

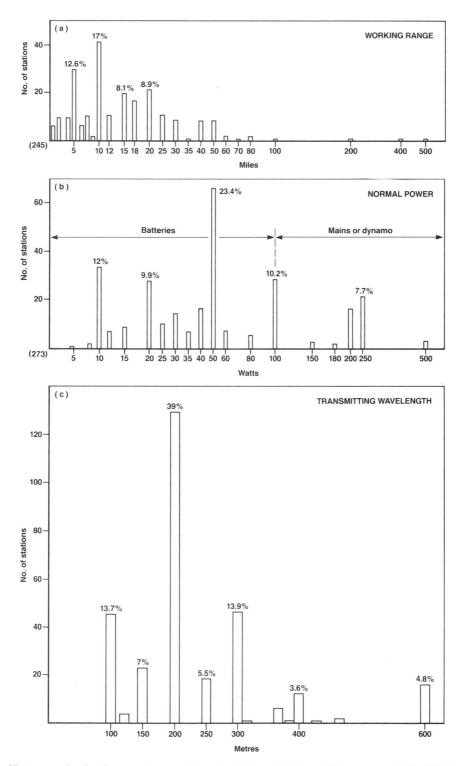

Histograms showing the range, power and wavelength of early stations which were recorded in *A W Gamage's Directory of Experimental Stations*.

supply of components; A W Gamage was later well-known for components, as were many others away from London.

Experimental stations were appearing in many of the larger centres of population where clubs were in existence, but in the London area, although there were a number of stations operating, there was no formal club. It was not until the General Post Office (GPO) indicated that they proposed to introduce some changes to the licences and pressure from club secretaries that there should be a national society that Rene Klein decided to propose the formation of a club in London.

A meeting was called and took place on 5th July 1913 at his home in West Hampstead, where it was decided to form the London Wireless Club. A press report of this meeting appeared in the *English Mechanic and World of Science* No. 2520, published on 11 July 1913.

❛ LONDON WIRELESS CLUB

At a meeting of wireless telegraphy amateurs held on Saturday 5th inst, an association was formed under the title of London Wireless Club for it's objects, the bringing together all amateurs interested in wireless telegraphy and telephony. The need for such a club has been apparent for some time and judging from the support promised and given will no doubt prove a success. The meeting being of an informal nature, it was decided to elect a temporary honorary secretary and treasurer, leaving the proper election of the committee to the general meeting, which will be held early in September next. The honorary secretary will be glad to hear from amateurs and will forward forms of application for membership. His address is Mr H Klein, Hon. Sec, (pro tem) 18 Crediton ❜ Road, West Hampstead N.W.

The formation of the London Wireless Club was also reported in a leader in the *London Daily News* on 9th July, 1913.

The timing of this meeting was fortuitous because within a few days of the formation of the club, the GPO advised all licence holders that, for the first time, a fee of £1.1s was to be charged to cover office expenses connected with the issue of each licence and inspection of the installation, but no annual royalty would be charged. At the same time they indicated that there would be no power limit applied to experimental stations generally. The power permitted would de-

pend in each case upon the character and locality of the installation.

Less than a week after the meeting, a meeting was requested by Klein for the GPO to receive a deputation from the club to discuss the ''new regulations affecting the issue of licences for experiments in wireless telegraphy''.

This meeting took place on 25th July, so establishing a contact between the issuing authority and the Society which has continued ever since. Although the delegation did not succeed in getting the proposed charge withdrawn, they did agree that licences would only be issued to bone fide experimenters.

Change of Name

The first General Meeting of the Club was held at Westminster School on the evening of Tuesday, 23rd September, 1913. Frank Hope-Jones was elected Chairman; Leslie McMichael, Vice-Chairman; Rene Klein, Honorary Secretary; and L.F. Fogarty, Honorary Treasurer.

At that meeting it was decided to appoint a Committee to draw up the Rules and Regulations of the Club. An Advisory Committee was also appointed to give advice to members on matters appertaining to the issue of transmitting and receiving licences and to negotiate with the G.P.O. on matters of mutual interest. The meeting also decided that there should be two grades of membership - Members and Associate Members. Full membership was restricted to persons over 21 years of age who had been engaged on experimental work for at least two years and/or had satisfied the Committee that they possessed the necessary qualifications and training. At the same time the name of the organisation was changed to the more dignified 'Wireless Society of London' (10th October, 1913).

Distinctive Call Signs.

In May 1910, the P.M.G. notified all licence holders that he had 'found it desirable to lay down a general rule that stations should have a distinctive call signal and that each station, when signalling, should begin each transmission with the call signal of the station with which it is desired to communicate and end with its own call signal.'

Mr. Klein was allotted the call RKX. Note: It was common practice to ask for one's initials, but there must be an 'X' somewhere in the three letters. Call signs were re-issued and some were duplicated.

THE LONDON WIRELESS CLUB.

18, CREDITON ROAD,

WEST HAMPSTEAD.

Sir,

In answer to your request, I beg to give you some particulars of the objects of the LONDON WIRELESS CLUB.

The Club has been formed in the first place to enable experimenters in Wireless Telegraphy and Telephony to meet, to exchange experiences, to read papers, and thereby further their knowledge in these branches of Science.

It is intended as soon as possible to erect a model wireless station for the purpose of demonstrating new apparatus and inventions.

Arrangements have been made whereby members can visit modern and efficient wireless stations already erected and obtain much useful information.

In the near future the Club intends acquiring a set of standard measuring and testing instruments, such as Wavemeters, Standard Inductances and Capacities, which will be available for members' use.

On presentation of their Membership cards, members will secure considerable reductions on the price of scientific instruments and materials for making their own apparatus.

Candidates for admission shall be persons who are interested in Wireless Telegraphy and Telephony, and shall, if approved by the Committee, be elected by general vote at an Ordinary Meeting of the Club.

SUBSCRIPTION.

The Subscription has been fixed at 10/6 per annum, which will include entrance fee for all members joining before the 8th of September, 1913.

Members elected after that date will pay an entrance fee of 2/6.

The subscription for country and foreign members has been fixed at 5/- per annum.

I enclose herewith an Application Form for Membership, and shall be pleased to receive same duly completed.

Yours faithfully,

R. H. KLEIN, *Hon. Sec.*

A printed letter of reply from *The London Wireless Club* of that time, relating the club's aims and aspirations and giving details of its subscription rates.

This Indenture made the *Twenty third*
day of *October* 191*3* BETWEEN A. W. GAMAGE
LIMITED whose registered office is at 107 Hatton Garden in the
County of London (who and whose successors and assigns are hereinafter wherever the context admits included in the term " Lessors ") of
the one part and

The Wireless Society of London

are hereinafter wherever the context admits included in the term
" Lessees ") of the other part WITNESSETH that in consideration of
the rent hereinafter reserved and of the covenants by the Lessees hereinafter contained the Lessors do hereby demise unto the Lessees ALL
THAT *Second floor of two rooms facing* ———
Hatton Garden. situate and
being *107 Hatton Garden* ——— in the County of
London TO HOLD the same until the Lessees for the term of
——— *one* ——— years from the *25th* ——— day of
December 191*3* subject to determination as hereinafter
mentioned YIELDING AND PAYING unto the Lessors the yearly
rent of £ *10 . 0 . 0 Ten Pounds* ———
——————————————————————→ by equal quarterly
payments on the usual quarter days the first payment to be made on
the *twenty fifth* ——— day of *March*
191*3* and to be the sum of £ *2 - 10 . 0* and the last quarterly
payment to be made in advance one calendar month before the expira-
tion of the term whether by effluxion of time or otherwise AND
YIELDING AND PAYING in the event of and immediately
upon the said term being determined by re-entry under the proviso

A copy of the agreement between A. W. Gamage Limited and the Wireless Society of London.

No. 2: H W Pope, PZX (later 3HT), South Norwood, London

Power: n/a

Wavelength: 450 metres

Range: 10 miles

At the time this picture was taken Pope was the wireless operator on the SS 'Crown Point' sailing out of Liverpool. The power control of his transmitter is the tap switch visible on the extreme right; the spark gap is a simple double-gap rotary type. The receiver used a two-crystal zincite-bornite detector; the large vertical inductance in the centre of the picture is a long-wave loading coil which was of 4 inches diameter and wound with 18 swg wire. It was fitted with a simple slider. All that is known about the aerial is that it was 80 feet long, although a counterpoise was almost certainly used

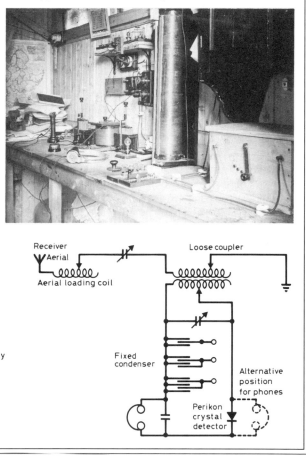

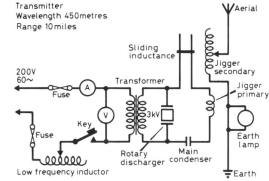

The Gamage Lease.

One of the greatest problems facing the founder members was that of finding suitable accommodation in Central London for the establishment of a Club station and meeting room.

On 11th July - only six days after the inaugural meeting - Leslie McMichael wrote to Messrs. A.W. Gamage Ltd. of High Holborn, requesting permission to exhibit a small notice in their Wireless Department drawing attention to the aims and objects of the Club. At that time the firm of Gamage carried large stocks of apparatus suitable for wireless experiments. Permission to exhibit the notice was granted.

As a result of informal discussions on the question of accommodation, Mr. A.W. Gamage (who was then the Managing Director) wrote personally to Mr. McMichael and offered to lease to the Club two

useful-size rooms above the firm's premises at 107 Hatton Garden. A nominal rent of £10 per annum was suggested. This generous offer was promptly accepted.

On 13th October 1913, an Agreement was signed between A.W. Gamage Ltd. and the Wireless Society of London. The first page of this historic document is reproduced herewith.

The newly acquired meeting place was soon fitted up with wireless equipment of all kinds and on 15th January 1914, an experimental licence was issued to the Society.

The terms and conditions under which that licence was granted make interesting reading; they were as follows:-

❝ It is understood that the Society would be willing to use a wavelength of 850 metres instead of the wavelength of 700 metres mentioned in your application; and the Lords Commissioners of the Admiralty stipulate that, before a licence is granted, a trial shall be carried out with the full power of half-kilowatt on the wavelength of 850 metres, in order to ascertain whether interference is caused with the reception of signals at the Admiralty station at Whitehall. I am accordingly to request that you will be good enough to state on what date and at what time you will be prepared to carry out such a test. Notice of not less than a week should be given, in order that the necessary arrangements may be made.

As it is the practice to fix a period of two hours per day (or two periods of one hour each) for the working of experimental stations on high power, you will perhaps be so good as to state the period or periods which would be suitable for the working of the station in question. In order to avoid interference with military wireless apparatus it will be a condition of the licence that the Society shall from time to time, communicate with the Commandant, Army Signal School, Aldershot, and obtain that officer's concurrence as to the arrangements to be made for the experiments.

It will also be stipulated in the licence that the apparatus shall only be worked by operators who have obtained the First or Second Class certificate of proficiency in radiotelegraphy issued by the Postmaster General.

I am to add that a general permission cannot be given to communicate with any members of the Society within a certain range. It is necessary for the stations with whom communication is authorised to be mentioned specifically in the licence; and, in accordance with the conditions applicable to licences for experiments, the number of stations with which a licensee is authorised to communicate is limited as a general rule to five, and in no case must exceed ten. I am to request, therefore, that you will be good enough to specify the stations, not exceeding ten in number, with which the Society wishes to be licensed to communicate, and to arrange for the licensees of those stations to forward their licences to this Office for amendment, reference being made to the registered number ❥ at the head of these papers.

A typical member's station might have been that

of J. Burton – the photograph was taken in November 1913 . . . .

J. Burton's private station: November, 1913.

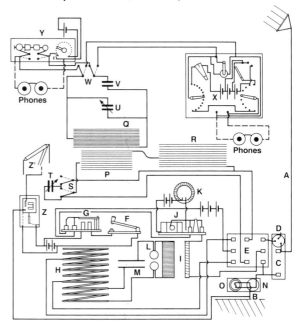

A diagram showing the general arrangement of the instruments.

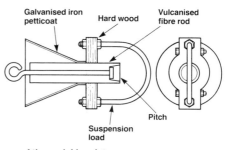

A diagram of the aerial insulator

No.3: Leslie McMichael, MXA (later 2FG), Forest Hill, London 1912

Power: 150W

Wavelength: 275 metres

Range: about 150 miles

McMichael was one of the four founder members of the London Wireless Club (see later). He first became interested in wireless in 1902, and in that year he succeeded in ringing a single-stroke railway bell at distances up to 200 yards. For these tests he used a transmitter with an 8 inch spark coil; the receiver detector used a coherer with silver and nickel filings.

After an interval of some ten years he returned to wireless in 1912, with the callsign MXA. The photograph shows the station at that time; the transmitter uses a 6 inch spark coil. The receiver consists of a large inductance with a slider for tuning and a 'Perikon'crystal detector. Its tuning range was up to 10,000 metres.

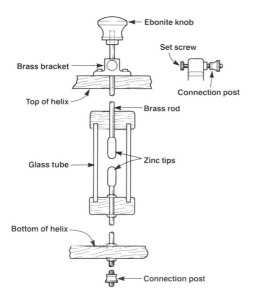

A diagram of the spark gap with muffler.

. . . . or the one belonging to Fred Cathery of Parkstone, Dorset

This compact station had a transmitter power of 10W on a wavelength of 100 metres, giving it a working range of 5-7 miles. Fred was apparently very interested in point-contact detectors: three of them can

be seen at the lower centre. This station seems to have been unusually neat and tidy for the period!

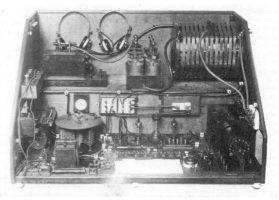

Fred Cathery's station at Parkstone, Dorset, 1913.

The Society was fortunate to have for its first President a highly respected engineer, Mr. A.A. Campbell-Swinton, well-known for his inventions, innovations and developments in electrical field, also it was he that first introduced Marconi to William Preece of the post Office in 1896, in a letter to *Nature* in 1908 he proposed a method 'Distant Electric Vision' using cathode Ray Tubes, the basis of modern television.

Before the end of 1913, the Society issued it's Rules

The 'Polaris' Case

In the early years of wireless it was natural that there should be patent protection, one which indirectly affected the amateur was the action against A. W. Gamage (well known supplier of wireless parts and simple receivers) by Marconi Wireless Telegraph Company. The High Court awarded damages and costs to Marconi and ordered Gamages to destroy the material already made.

The patents concerned were No.13636 of 1913, issued to Marconi W. T. Co. and C. S. Franklin; the other was No. 28413 of 1913, issued to Marconi W. T. Co. and H. J. Round.

Both of these patents referred to the principle of reaction, the latter being directly applicable to experimenters, these patents were known as the 'POLARIS' patents.

Circuit diagrams from the original patents are shown here.

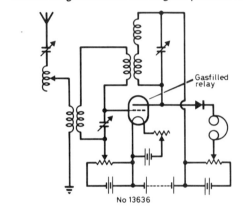

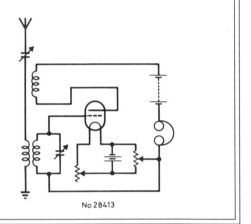

(constitution) and list of members in a small booklet to members.

At the Inaugural meeting of the Society on 21st January 1914 at the Institution of Electrical Engineers, during the Presidential address, a greetings message was sent from the Eiffel Tower station in Paris by Commandant Ferrie, who had been elected a Vice-President. It said:

> Commandant Ferrie presents his compliments to the President and his distinguished colleagues of the Wireless Society of London, and assures them of his sincere good wishes (ses sincere sympathies). Long live England and long live the Entente Cordiale.

On 1st August 1914 the Government decreed that stations should be closed down and sent telegrams to all registered amateurs instructing them to dismantle their apparatus. Amateur equipment was sealed up and mostly removed and by the end of September World War I had begun.

Although this meant total cessation of experimental activity for the duration, it also implied that many people were to be trained in the art of wireless telegraphy by the armed services and that a great deal of military equipment would shortly come on to the surplus market at very low prices.

The expertise of the pre-war amateurs proved of immense value to the armed forces; one outstanding

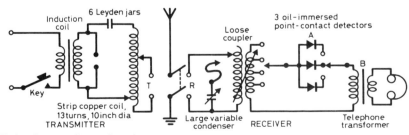

A diagram of Fred Cathery's transmitter and receiver.

POST OFFICE TELEGRAPHS.

N.B.—This Form must accompany any inquiry respecting this Telegram.

If the Receiver of an Inland Telegram doubts its accuracy, he may have it repeated on payment of half the amount originally paid for its transmission, any fraction of 1d. less than ½d. being reckoned as ½d.; and if it be found that there was any inaccuracy, the amount paid for repetition will be refunded. Special conditions are applicable to the repetition of Foreign Telegrams.

Office of Origin and Service Instructions.

Office Stamp.

Charges to pay

s.　d.

Central Telegraph Office Handed in at 7 0¹ Received here at 7·26¹

TO: A. T. Lee Lonsdale Hill Lonsdale Place Derby

In accordance with your wireless licence postmaster general requires you to remove at once your aerial wires and dismantle your apparatus at each of its stations one of his officers

POST OFFICE TELEGRAPHS.

N.B.—This Form must accompany any inquiry respecting this Telegram.

If the Receiver of an Inland Telegram doubts its accuracy, he may have it repeated on payment of half the amount originally paid for its transmission, any fraction of 1d. less than ½d. being reckoned as ½d.; and if it be found that there was any inaccuracy, the amount paid for repetition will be refunded. Special conditions are applicable to the repetition of Foreign Telegrams.

Office of Origin and Service Instructions.

Office Stamp.

Charges to pay

s.　d.

Handed in at .M., Received here at .M.

TO: Lee

will shortly call upon you Secretary Postoffice

The Post Office telegram sent to all registered amateur radio operators closing down their stations at the outbreak of World War I.

W. E. F. Corsham, later 2UV.

example was W E F ('Bill') Corsham, later 2UV, who although aged only 14 at the beginning of the war spent most of it as a wireless inspector/instructor at Bletchley serving with the Royal Engineers.

Chapter 2

The Interwar Years

During the months following the end of World War I, interest in wireless on the part of both the general public and experimenters grew considerably. However, the authorities initially refused to issue any kind of licence for either transmission or reception, and in spite of a vigorous press campaign the situation remained unchanged. How much this was connected with the GPO's monopoly on communications and how much was concerned with the possible use of radio for subversive activities is not clear. In November 1919 the magazine *Wireless World* published a supplement entitled *The Amateur Position* - incidentally, it is worth mentioning that at this period the word 'amateur' was not only applied to the experimenter who wished to transmit but also to those who merely wished to listen and construct their own receivers. This supplement carried the Government's proposals for authorisation of the '. . . . use of wireless apparatus for reception of signals'. However, '. . . . No licence or permission to transmit by wireless telegraphy is at present obtainable by amateurs, as the conditions under which this will be allowed are not yet settled'.

In the course of a conference in February 1920 it was announced that Authority had relented slightly and was now prepared to issue 10W licences to approved applicants. However, these '. . . . will not be granted for mere intercommunication purposes'.

The new transmitting licences were hedged about with many restrictions, including one which stated, '. . . . Communication will be authorized only with specified stations and not exceeding five in number.' Power input was limited to 10W except with special permission; artificial aerial licences would be issued for experiments not requiring the use of a radiating aerial. Some definite object of scientific value or

Card of Authority to conduct experiments with portable wireless telegraph apparatus.

Issued by order of the Postmaster General.

GENERAL POST OFFICE, LONDON,
January 1920

The bearer, Mr. *C. L. Drury*

of *1349 Almond St Derby*

has been licensed by the Postmaster General to conduct experiments with portable wireless apparatus within a radius of *10* miles of *above address*

for the Secretary.

This card must be carried whenever experiments are being made with portable wireless telegraph apparatus and produced for inspection when required.

The Post Office's 'Card of Authority' for portable operation. This permit was prior to the licences issued in February, 1920.

Early Receiving Stations

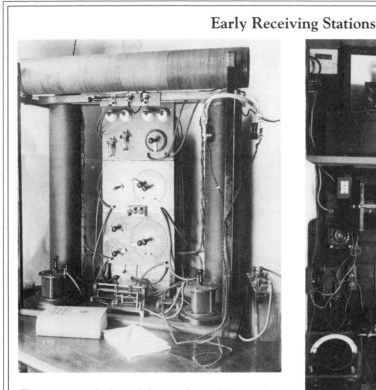

These two typical receiving stations of the early twenties illustrate differences in construction, particularly in respect of the tuning method used. At this period 'short waves' meant wavelengths of between about 440 and 600 metres for the reception of ships and coastal stations. Other stations operated on 'long waves' up to about 20,000 metres. Amateurs operated on 440 and 1,000 metres, but in the London area interference with traffic to and from Croydon Aerodrome caused suspension of amateur operation on that wavelength.

In Mitchell's station (left), tuning was largely by means of tapped inductance and two 0.001 mF condensers were used as trimmers. No tuning dials were fitted. He also used two V24 valves as HF amplifiers.

Ison's station (right) used loose couplers with loading coils and sliders, with a switched tap for the inner coil. He also had a two-stage HF amplifier and two additional valves for use as LF amplifiers ('note magnifiers').

It's worth remembering that the use of reaction had not yet become popular and that a valve detector stage was not much better than a crystal detector except that it was more stable.

general public utility had to be shown, and restrictions were placed on wavelengths and hours of working. Bands were 1,000 and 180 metres. As a result of specific proposals put forward by the Society, however, some of these restrictions gradually disappeared.

More months were to pass before the coveted licences were issued. However, as the autumn of 1920 approached, approved applicants began to receive their permits; each was allotted a callsign comprising a number (at first 2 but soon also 5 or 6) followed by two letters - most of the pre-war three-letter calls had been silenced for ever. Many of the new calls were first formed from initials or names

Another significant event of 1920 was that Guglielmo Marconi, GCVO, DSc, LL.D, was made an Honorary Member of the Society in that year

Guglielmo Marconi, GCVO, DSc, LL.D, was made an Honorary Member of the Society in 1920.

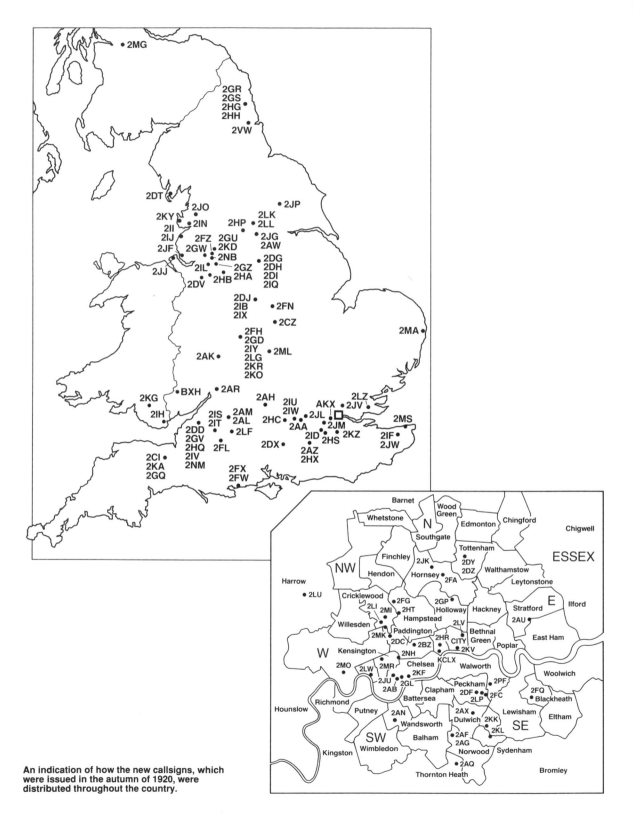

An indication of how the new callsigns, which were issued in the autumn of 1920, were distributed throughout the country.

E. J (Ernest) Simmonds, 2OD

E J Simmonds, 2OD, of Gerrards Cross, a Bank Manager by profession, was amongst the most active experimenters in the early twenties. In addition to having a number of successful long-distance contacts, his equipment was constantly being developed and he wrote many articles about it.

Like most of his contemporaries, Simmonds started as a listener; the photograph below shows his receiving station, which was typical of the period.

The central feature was the large aerial tuning inductance. By 1922 he was using a superheterodyne receiver and indeed he published a detailed description of it. Simmond's receiver did not employ a beat frequency oscillator; instead it relied on making the middle stage of the IF amplifier oscillate by adjusting its bias. The circuit of the receiver is shown below.

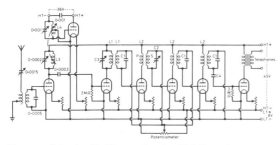

The complete circuit of the receiver in which the values are as follows: C1 0.0001 mfd., C2 0.0005 mfd., C3 0.0002 mfd., C4 0.0003 mfd., L1 800 turns 36 D.S.C., L2 Primary 400 turns, Secondary 800 turns, 36 D.S.C., L3 Tuned anode coil, L4 Threepin plug-in oscillator coil. Accummulator power was used for both filament and anode supplies to reduce the possibility of mains-borne interference.

From the point of view of the 1980s it is striking that the superhet went out of favour so early, to be replaced by the classic 0-V-1. Here again Simmonds was one of the first to publish a description of a 'Modern Short Wave Receiver', in which a tubular DEV valve was used as the detector and there was a transformer - coupled low-frequency stage.

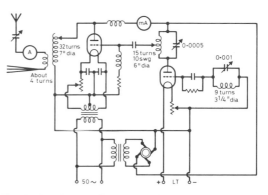

The circuit makes use of a master oscillator and some practical details are given of the construction of the tuning inductances. The output terminals of the synchronous rectifier should be bridged with a suitable smothing condenser whilst an H.F. choke may with advantage be connected in the lead to the valve plates.

On the transmitting side, Simmonds was also a prolific experimenter. He soon graduated from the single-valve transmitter to a master oscillator arrangement, using valves such as the Mullard 0/150 and 0/250; the circuit of a typical arrangement is shown above and the apparatus itself below.

continued on next page

continueud from preceding page

Simmonds was fortunate enough to have an AC supply available and he used a home-constructed rotary rectifier. This apparently gave good service and certainly gave his signal a distinctive note. Later he changed to an accumulator HT supply, which can be seen on the right-hand side of the picture below, in an attempt to achieve the much sought-after 'pure DC note'. For an aerial, Simmonds used a simple cage type, with counterpoise.

The picture at the top of the next column shows Simmond's station in 1923, with a 115 metre transmitter and superhet receiver.

His station in later years is shown in the picture below.

Transatlantic Tests

During the summer of 1920, reports of long-distance working led amateurs to speculate whether the Atlantic could be bridged on 200 metres and below. Philip Coursey, 2JK, a prominent member of the Society, planned tests to take place in February 1921. Although a considerable number of members took part, no signals could be identified. The failure was attributed to the short duration (three minutes) of the test trans-

missions from American stations and also interference from the harmonics of high-power commercial stations. Nevertheless, considerable interest was gener-

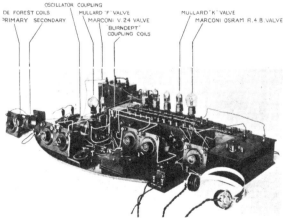

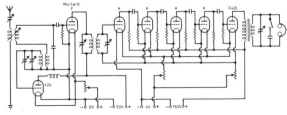

R. D. Wade's seven-valve receiver which took part in the initial transatlantic tests, details of which were later published.

ated and a further series of tests was planned to take place between 8 and 17 December 1921.

Circuit details of two stations which had taken part in the initial tests were published, those of W R Wade of Clifton and the Glasgow & District Radio Club. Wade's seven-valve receiver consisted of a detector with a separate local oscillator tuned to a wavelength of about 3,000 metres. This fed a five-stage RC-coupled amplifier. The second detector was an R4b soft valve transformer-coupled to the headphones. In order to keep the receiver on the correct wavelength a separate calibration oscillator was available. Construction of the receiver was carried out by Wade and M L Megson, of the Wireless Society of London and chairman of the Manchester Radio & Scientific Society. The aerial was an inverted L with a twin-wire top 45ft long with 9ft spreaders at 50ft. A buried wire counterpoise was available.

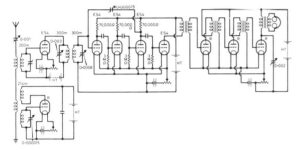

Circuit arrangement used by the Glasgow & District Radio Club when taking part in the transatlantic tests, details of which were also published later.

The Glasgow club's receiver (see circuit diagram above) was almost the same as Wade's but with a two-

stage low-frequency amplifier; some regeneration was provided in the IF amplifier. Unfortunately no photograph is available.

In a piece published in the American magazine QST after the failure of the tests, the Americans were somewhat disparaging about British ability to copy DX stations. For the second set of tests Paul Godley came over from America and set up a receiving station at Ardrossan, Scotland. A circuit diagram of his receiver is shown at the foot of this page together with the arrangement of the Beverage antenna – the first to be used in the UK. The receiver was an early American superhet with an RC-coupled IF amplifier and a regenerative first detector. With this American high-tech approach Godley identified signals from 1BCG on 9 December and copied a complete message on the 12th. However, the sting in the tail was that the British station 2KW had copied no less than seven American stations; to rub salt into the wound 2KW made the first positive identification of an American station on 8 December, a day before Godley heard 1BCG!

W F Burne, 2KW, of the Manchester Wireless Society, was the hero of the hour. His aerial consisted of a 45ft inverted-L (in contrast to Godley's massive Beverage) at a height of 45ft, with a 50ft twin-wire lead-in.

The receiver together with the circuit diagram is shown on the next page; it consisted of a Mark III tuner followed by six stages of HF transformer-coupled amplifiers with a tuning range of 180-325 metres, using home-made variable condensers.

A separate heterodyne oscillator was coupled to the detector, thus providing a considerable degree of isolation

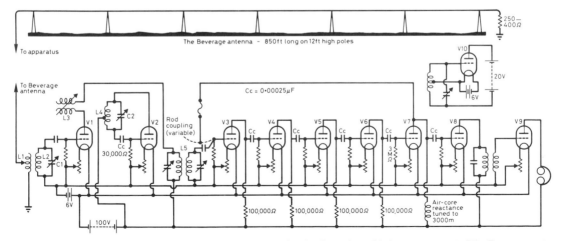

A circuit diagram of Paul Godley's receiving station at Ardrossan, Scotland together with the arrangement of the Beverage antenna.

W. F. Burn's aerial consisted of a 45ft. inverted 'L' with a 50ft. twin-wire lead-in.

from the aerial and making it unlikely that the receiver would cause interference to other stations. A single-stage LF amplifier which could be switched in or out completed the installation.

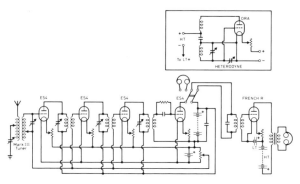

A circuit diagram of W. F. Burne's receiver.

H H Whitfield, 2LG, of Hall Green, Birmingham, was the next most successful station to receive trans-atlantic signals. His aerial was similar to that used by Burne but his receiver was significantly different. The circuit diagram is shown in the next column. In the first valve stage, the anode tuned circuit was coupled

W. F. Burn's receiver.

directly to the grid and aerial circuits. Self-oscillation was claimed to be prevented by

a) connecting the grid to the negative side of the filament battery and
b) 'reverse winding the anode coil'(!).

A separate heterodyne oscillator was used; it was about 18 inches away from the receiver.

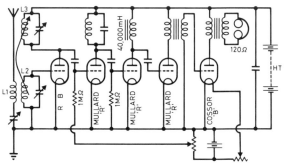

A circuit diagram of H. H. Whitfield's receiver.

The next challenge was obviously two-way working. Tests took place in December 1922 and two major stations took part; the Manchester Radio Society's 5MS and the Society's own station 5WS, set up for the purpose at Wandsworth. This had a special licence permitting 1 kW input. Various views of 5WS are shown on page 30, together with a circuit diagram. The 5MS tranmitter circuit diagram is also shown on page 30.

On page 29, together with the 5MS transmitter, is a photograph of the elaborate aerial array which was used. 5MS was also licensed to run 1 kW. The full story of these tests can be read in *World at their Fingertips*; it must suffice to say here that no-one could be quite sure which station was the first to be heard in America! It is worth mentioning that the Manchester transmitter was a much more workman-

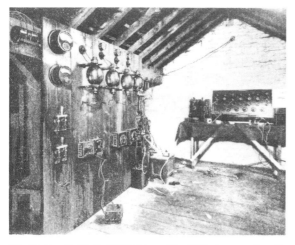

Manchester Radio Society's transmitter 5MS above and on the right the elaborate aerial array which was used.

✧

Below: the committee which was responsible for the first-ever all British wireless exhibition and convention, the agreement of the Prince of Wales to become patron of the Wireless Society of London, and the change of name of the Wireless Society of London to the Radio Society of Great Britain.

loaned by Marconi for the tests. A large six-wire aerial was supported by two 80ft masts fed at one end by a six-wire feeder; the aerial current was said to be 9A under normal conditions. The Manchester receiver was apparently an early superheterodyne, with the detector and oscillator being built into the tuner and the main HF amplifier and second detector being a seven-valve unit using R valves.

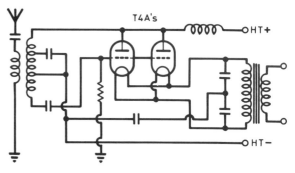

A circuit diagram of the Society's transmitter 5WS.

Briefly returning to October/November 1922, three notable events occurred. The first was the first-ever all British wireless exhibition and convention. The second was the agreement of the Prince of Wales to become patron of the Wireless Society of London; the third was the change of name on the part of the latter body to the 'Radio Society of Great Britain'. The photograph on page 29 shows the committee which was responsible for these developments.

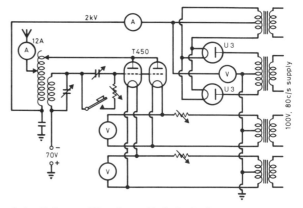

A circuit digram of Manchester Radio Society's transmitter 5MS.

Two views of the Society's transmitter 5WS.

like affair than the Society's, which had an air of having been rather hastily assembled for the event. It was a self-oscillator, with a pair of T4A triodes in parallel and a pair of U2 rectifiers, which had been

Chapter 3

Five Notable Stations (1922 – 1924)

W K Alford, 2DX (formerly TXK)

Alford had some advantage over many of his contemporaries, having started his wireless activities in 1910 and being first licensed in 1912. At first he used spark transmitters and the then popular crystal receiver covering wavelengths up to 10,000 metres. When he obtained his new licence in March 1919 he was well placed to pick up the new techniques involving the use of thermionic valves for both transmitting and receiving purposes. A description of his first station was published in the July 1923 edition of Modern Wireless and it is shown at the foot of the page. At this time the aerial consisted of two four-wire cages 50ft long at 50ft above the ground.

The transmitter makes use of three R-type valves apparently connected in parallel. Speech modulation was either by the so- called 'direct method' in the aerial circuit or the 'grid leak' method. The operating wavelength was 195 metres. The power supply was provided by a gas engine built before World War I from castings; this drove a dynamo for charging accumulators and supplying the high-voltage transformer.

The receiver is interesting insofar as it was one of the first home-constructed superheterodynes. This version had 10 valves, most of which were used in the 'long wave amplifier' operating on 3,000 metres. With this receiver it was claimed that signals could be equally well received on the frame aerial as on an outside aerial.

By October 1924 the transmitter had been completely rebuilt (see next page). It now consisted of a

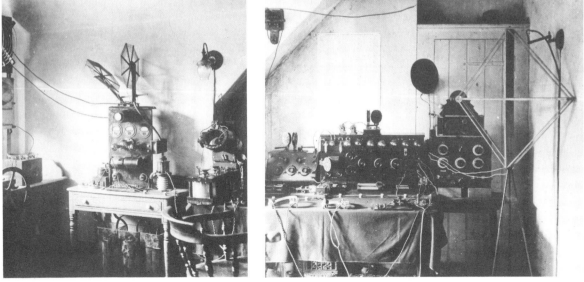

W. K. Alford's first station, a description of which was published in the July 1923 edition of Modern Wireless.

The 90 metre transmitter which was re-built in 1924.

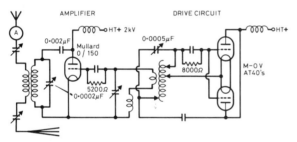

A circuit diagram of the re-built transmitter.

master oscillator with two AT40 valves in parallel driving a Mullard 0/150 valve amplifier with 2 kV on

The receiver which Alford built for Gerald Marcuse, 2NM.

The superheterodyne receiver.

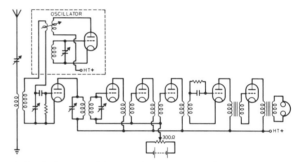

A circuit diagram of the superheterodyne receiver.

the anode. Rectification was carried out by a pair of Mullard U50 half-wave rectifiers. The transmitter was tunable between 70 and 120 metres. The receiver was unchanged except that its tuning range had been extended to permit reception of the Eiffel Tower calibration signals on 25 metres; a photograph of the receiver is shown above this column and also the circuit diagram.

It is worth recording that, as a result of the considerable success of this receiver, Alford built another version for his great friend Gerald Marcuse, 2NM. This magnificent creation is shown on the left, it used tubular V24 valves and was a prominent feature of early pictures of 2NM's station.

✧   ✧   ✧

W E F Corsham, 2UV (Uncle Vic)

Bill, who had spent most of the 14-18 war as a wireless inspector/instructor at Bletchley in the RESS, placed him in a good position to take up experimental work on his own account later.

During his service he had handled most types of army equipment, particularly spark and valve transmitters, together with a wide range of receivers.

He may be regarded as a classic case of making the most of very little. At the time of the first successful transatlantic tests he was fortunate enough to meet Godley, the ARRL representative, while he was in Wembley before moving to Ardrossan in Scotland. Using a very simple 3 valve receiver, he was able to receive signals from America and shared third prize with 2JZ (Aberdeen). Initially he had had some difficulty in obtaining even a receiving licence, which was not granted until June 1921.

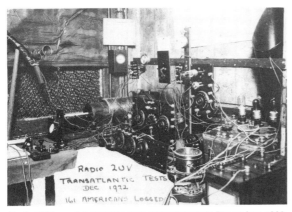

Radio 2UV, used during the transatlantic tests in December, 1922.

He was greatly concerned (if not alarmed) at the proliferation of amateur organisations growing up in and around London, he was at the time a member of the Amateur Radio Research Association (ARRA) and the British Wireless Relay League (BWRL). There was also the Radio Transmitters Society (RTS). He felt that it was important for all these smaller units to come together with the Wireless Society of London if they were to get anywhere with the authorities. After considerable discussion, the smaller units were absorbed into the parent organisation by forming the T&R section, which initially was a separate section and had its own membership.

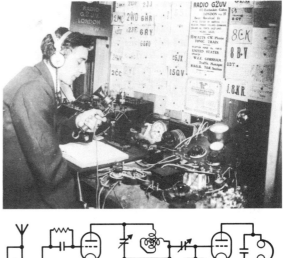

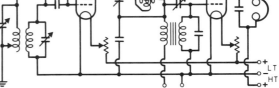

A photograph and circuit diagram of one of Bill Corsham's receivers which had an unusual form of reaction, using a variometer for the adjustment of inductance in the anode circuit, in place of the normal feedback coil and condenser, claimed to have given a smoother control. This type of circuit was later used in some commercial broadcast receivers.

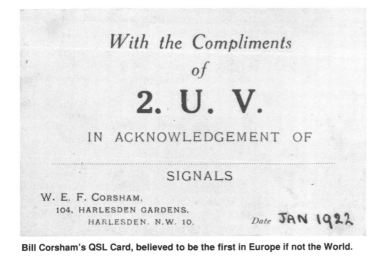

Bill Corsham's QSL Card, believed to be the first in Europe if not the World.

In January 1922 he produced what is believed to be the first QSL card, certainly in Europe if not in the World; a full sized copy is reproduced on the left of the page.

His transmissions were by Spark, Tonic Train, C.W. and telephony, the latter was mainly of gramophone records apart from speech, but occasionally live transmission by budding local talent. At all times in the early days his power was always low, having to operate from accumulators and dry batteries or a hand driven generator for H.T. until eventually the mains arrived.

Operation was on all the then recognised wavelengths; 100 metres soon

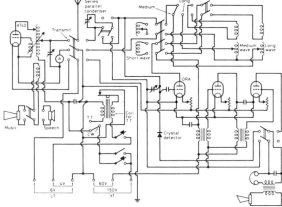

A photograph and circuit diagram showing another of Bill Corsham's creations.

became withdrawn owing to interference with Croydon aerodrome. Following the successful outcome of the transatlantic tests he regularly made contact with 2JZ in Aberdeen on 180 metres. It was during these tests, that a great deal of attention was gained because he was able to copy the Aberdeen station when practically no-one else in the South could. This turned out to be because his receiver had been so carefully adjusted

that its sensitivity was well above average. Throughout his early operations he was very often handicapped by serious interference from harmonics from GFA GKB stations.

In the Spring of 1924 when the Society's members were giving regular talks broadcast from 2LO, W E Corsham, 2UV, was asked at short notice to take over a talk to have been given by Gerry Marcuse, the script of which had been approved, was changed at the end (without approval). He said:-

> ❝ In conclusion, I would like to make a few remarks about experiments with overseas stations. Numbers of our stations have been in constant communication with amateurs in all parts of North America, Canada, France, Belgium, Holland, Denmark, Switzerland, Luxembourg, Italy, Norway and Finland, which I think you will agree are excellent performances. The recent reception by 2OD and myself of South American amateurs has opened up a new field and brings the prospect of communication at a distance of 7000 miles much nearer, especially as 2OD has been heard in California, and French 8AB in Brazil.
>
> So the amateur goes on from success to success, and I have no doubt that in the very near future we shall be able to place on record the reception of an amateur station in Australia. Certainly a very formidable task, but one which the amateur is even now tackling in his usual optimistic manner.
>
> Perhaps, therefore, the day when the British amateur will have encircled the world is not so far ahead after all. ❞

This statement was made to provoke the authorities to take some action, at the time communication with overseas station was not permitted, it could have lead to cancellation of licences, in the event the authorities modified the licence conditions, so that amateur progress was maintain unhindered.

✧   ✧   ✧

H. S. Walker, 2OM (formerly AKX)

Like Alford, Walker came back to amateur wireless after the war; he had served in the signals section of the Army in France. Walker foresaw the tremendous potential of broadcasting and his interest in telephony expressed itself in regular music broadcasts. He had a considerable listener following of his gramophone

Eric Megaw, G6MU, Belfast

Eric was extremely interested in the generation of very high frequencies and a great supporter of the Society in his early days. He studied the Barkhousen-Kurz and the Gill-Morrell electron coupled methods and later went on to the development of magnetrons.

His first interest in this type of valve was for higher power on 'metre waves'. The first production design, the CW10, gave 50 watts on 2 metres, it was a simple split (two) anode type; later four anode and others were made. The illustration shows a four anode type.

It is likely that his work on multi-anode types provided, eventually, the basic idea to Randell and Boot for their invention of the resonant cavity magnetron for high power pulse which was used so successfully in the later British Radar during world war II.

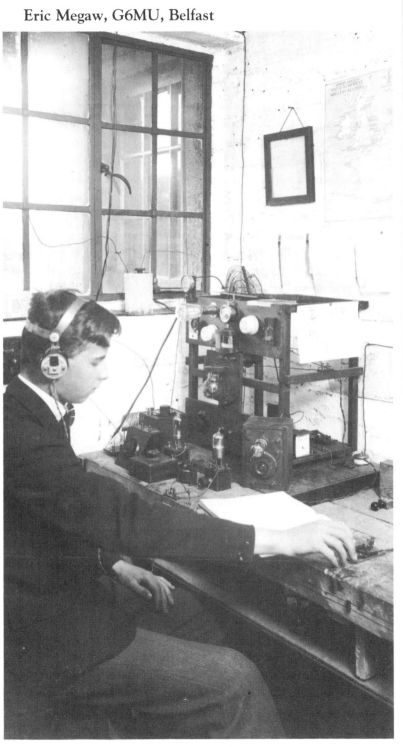

record programmes on Sunday mornings, always commencing transmissions with 'This is Brentford calling'! The transmission was audible over most parts of West London.

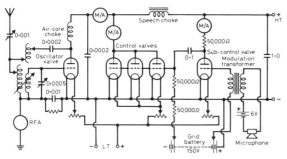

A typical choke-control transmitter.

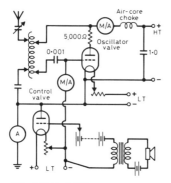

The grid leak method of modulation.

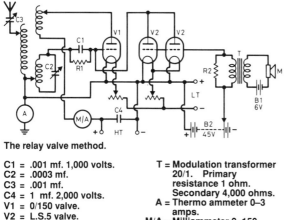

The relay valve method.

C1 = .001 mf. 1,000 volts.	T = Modulation transformer 20/1. Primary resistance 1 ohm. Secondary 4,000 ohms.
C2 = .0003 mf.	
C3 = .001 mf.	
C4 = 1 mf. 2,000 volts.	
V1 = 0/150 valve.	A = Thermo ammeter 0–3 amps.
V2 = L.S.5 valve.	
B1 = 6-volt battery.	M/A = Milliammeter 0–150 milliamps.
B2 = 45-volt tapped grid battery.	M = High-resistance microphone.
R1 = 5,000 ohms.	L.T. = 12 volts.
R2 = 50,000 ohms.	H.T. = 1,500 volts.

Walker was one of the founders of the Radio Communication Company, a widely respected equipment manufacturer of the early days. This company was one of the original six which formed the British Broadcasting Company (BBC).

His main interest was the transmission of high-quality speech and music, and in August 1924 he published an article in the magazine *Experimental Wireless* which described the classic choke-modulation circuit. Walker also drew attention to the need for a modulator stage to have a higher power rating than the oscillator to provide anything like full modulation. Also described was his patented 'Relay' method of grid modulation (British Patent No 188,483 of 1921) which was shown to be very efficient.

A typical transmitter as used by H. S. Walker.

Walker later joined the BBC as Engineer-in-Charge at Bournemouth and he later became Valve Controller for the Corporation.

✧   ✧   ✧

Jack Partridge, 2KF

Partridge was the first British amateur to make two-way contact with America on 200 metres; the other station was 1MO operated by K B Warner at the American Radio Relay League headquarters at Hartford, Conn. It is interesting to note that both stations were using simple two-valve 0-V-1 receivers and preferred them to superheterodyne types: also, both felt that the best results were obtained with an HT voltage of not more than 60. The transmitter at 2KF was the usual single-valve power oscillator, in this case using a Mullard 0/150 valve with 1.5 kV on the anode. This voltage was derived from a motor-generator set using the domestic 100V DC supply for the motor.

From the circuit diagram it appears that the anode

coil had the full voltage on it and therefore the aerial must have been fully insulated. The aerial itself was a typical L type having three wires 60ft long in parallel at a height of 50ft. A five-wire counterpoise mounted some 7ft above ground was part of the radiating system. A separate copper plate earth was also used.

2KF, a well-known telephony station.

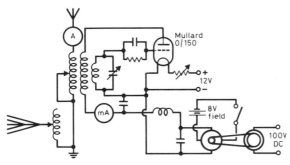

The circuit diagram of transmitter 2KF.

Although no details of the modulation arrangements are available, 2KF was a well-known telephony

Jack Partridge, 2KF.

station. There is a two-valve microphone amplifier using LS5 valves visible in and it is almost certain that grid modulation would have been used. Partridge was one of the well-known 'London broadcasters' along with 2OM, 2UV, etc, whose broadcasts were a regular Sunday-morning feature.

Partridge later became involved with the Marconi Company in its shortwave relay of the opening of the Empire Exhibition at Wembley in 1924.

✧   ✧   ✧

E H Robinson, 2VW.

This station was one of the early transmitters of speech and music, and Robinson was probably the first person to record transmissions from other stations on an Edison Bell-type cylinder machine in 1922. He was an avid experimenter and innovator, probably best known for his work with chemical rectification of AC mains for anode supplies.

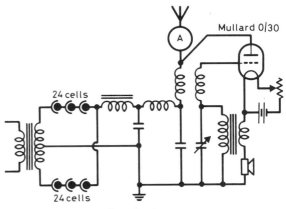

E. H. Robinson's transmitter circuit.

In the early twenties the only thermionic rectifiers available were for high-power use and were quite unsuitable for the average experimenter. This meant that other means of rectification were needed, and at the time the choice fell between:

a) the synchronous mechanical rectifier, which required precision construction and which was very noisy in operation or

b) the chemical rectifier, which was silent and could be readily constructed from easily available materials. It was, however, rather messy, and if care was not taken the corrosive fumes could damage other equipment.

Descriptions of chemical rectifiers published in the

These pictures (above and right) illustrate the formidable 'chemical recitifier' stack, the published descriptions of which were eagerly awaited by constructors.

journals of the day were eagerly awaited by constructors; incidentally, the construction of suitable transformers was often included since these were not normally available either. The rectifier consisted of an aluminium wire and an iron wire, both 16 swg, dipped into a saturated solution of ammonium phosphate to a depth of about 1 inch. A layer of paraffin oil was poured over the surface of the electrolyte to reduce fumes from the rectifier when in operation!

It was usual to use 24 'cells' in each leg of the rectifier for operation at around 500V; the cells normally consisted of $5/8$ of an inch diameter test tubes.

Two photographs showing detalis of E. H. Robinson's station, which was one of the early transmitters used for speech and music.

Chapter 4

Early Mobiles

In preparation for the opening of the British Empire Exhibition at Wembley in 1924, the Marconi Company had installed a Shortwave relay transmitter, but were having trouble with valve failures and appealed for an experienced shortwave radio enthusiast to operate this transmitter. Of those approached, 2OM, 2KF, 2WJ and 5BV, only Partridge 2KF was available. He successfully ran the transmitter without any further trouble. This episode resulted in Jack being permanently employed at Tatsfield monitoring station.

By 1923 there was a great deal of interest in telephony, and it is notable that the GPO ceased issuing licences for spark transmission in 1924.

In the summer of 1924 the Society, in co-operation with the London & North Eastern Railway, set up a short-wave transmitter and receiver in a luggage van attached to the relief part of the 7.30 'Scotch express', leaving London's King's Cross station at 7.38pm. The callsign used was 6ZZ.

The preceding photograph which has been reproduced in various publications, purports to show the express leaving King's Cross station with the experimental transmitter and receiver. In point of fact it shows the departure of the inaugural 'Sheffield Pullman' at 11.5 am on 2 June 1924; the locomotive is Ivatt 'Large Atlantic' (LNER Class C1) No 4426 in the hands of Driver Tommy Topliss. However, we do have some slightly more authentic photographs, such as those on the next page.

The aerial for the tests was slung near the roof; it consisted of two wires 50ft long spaced 6 inches apart and joined together at the far end via a hot-wire aerial ammeter. At the other end the wires were attached to the side walls of the van with one end connected to the equipment, thus forming an end-fed aerial. The transmitter was a single-valve self-oscillator using a Mullard 0/150A low impedance triode with 1 kV on the anode

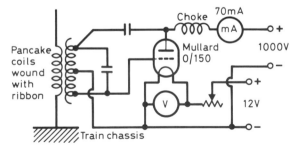

A circuit diagram of the transmitter 6ZZ.

It seems a pity in retrospect that no form of modulation was provided. The wavelength chosen was 185.2 metres, which was close to the second harmonic of 2LO (182.5m). On the receiving side the two receivers used were well-tried designs, both of which had been published in *Wireless World* .

The Ivatt 'Large Atlantic' (LNER Class C1) No 4426 in the hands of Driver Tommy Topliss.

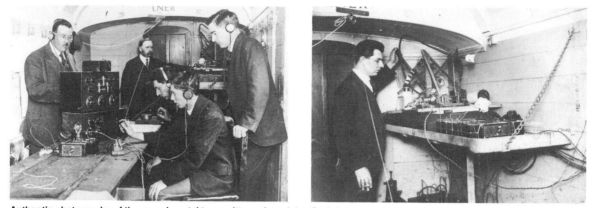

Authentic photographs of the experimental transmitter onboard the 'Scotch express' in the summer of 1924.

Contact stations along the route had been arranged in advance. They were 2WD at Bedford, 5DN at Sheffield, 2DR at Shipley, Yorks, 2OG in York and 5MO at Rowlands Gill. Signals were received from as far south as Huntingdon by 5MO. From the results obtained it was concluded that signals could be received from the train at ranges of about 100 miles provided that it was not in a tunnel or deep cutting.

One member of the 'train team' was L McMichael, 2FG, and for interest here is a picture, in the next column, of his home station at that time. The unit on the right is a combined transmitter and receiver; the right-hand section contains the transmitter, which comprises a self-oscillator and a modulator which appear to use Mullard O/30 valves. Two HT rectifier valves are seen below. The station appears to contain two Post-Office-type microphones. The left-hand section contains a five-valve receiver using R valves in a 2-V-2 configuration.

1925 was an eventful year for the Society. In April a conference of national amateur radio societies took place in Paris, and the RSGB delegation was very much involved with the creation of the International Amateur Radio Union. The RSGB honorary secretary,

Gerald Marcuse, 2NM, was elected Vice-President, with the ARRL president, Hiram P Maxim, being elected President.

A picture of L. McMichael's home station.

On the next page is a photograph of four officials present at this meeting. One member of the RSGB delegation was Hugh Ryan, 5BV, who was made chairman of one of the committees because he was able to speak and write in French.

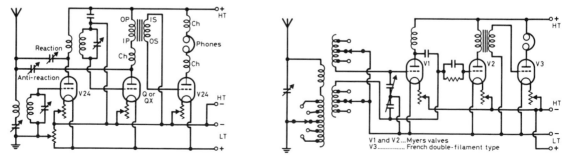

Circuit diagrams of the two receivers which were used. V1 and V2 were Myers valves, V3 was a French double filament type.

The picture on the right is a photograph of his station; the transmitter is a single-valve self-excited oscillator using an O/150 and another valve is mounted adjacent to it as a spare. The large vertical coil is wound with copper ribbon. Ryan contributed a DX commentary in *Experimental Wireless* magazine for many months, beginning in December 1924.

Four officials who were present at the conference of national amateur radio societies which took place in Paris in April, 1925. From left to right they are: J. G. Mezyer, Hiram P. Maxim, Gerald Marcuse and Kenneth B. Warner.

In July of the same year the first edition of the *T & R Bulletin* appeared, and the picture below shows the diligent staff at work on a *Bull* issue.

Preparing the *Bull* at 53 Victoria Street, London, c. 1928.

On the next page is a picture of the *Bull's* first editor, J A J Cooper, 5TR, with what appears to be a beautifully constructed TPTG transmitter using an LS5 valve. Initially the *T & R Bulletin* was for members of that section but later it became the journal of the

Hugh Ryan 5BV, of Wimbledon, London, sitting at his station.

Society proper. As such its first editor was G Thomas, 5YK, assisted by J Matthews, 6LL, D Chisholm,, 2CX, J Curnow, 6CW and A Milne, 2MI.

J. A. J. Cooper 5TR, first editor of the Bull, 1925.

✧ ✧ ✧

Was It the First?

In *Wireless World* for 25 August 1926 Freddie Haynes, 2DY, described what may have been the first-ever transceiver; This handsome device is illustrated on the next page with its internals.

The Radio Society Badges

The illustration on the left shows the badge originally adopted by the Society, dating from October 1924. It was a combination of two designs submitted by Messrs H W Taylor and H H Townley in response to a competition, and it was chosen by a committee consisting of Admiral of the Fleet Sir Henry Jackson, A A Campbell-Swinton and the President, Dr W H Eccles. Later, the diamond, shown on he right, was introduced for the 'T & R section' and for many years both badges were current. It should be remembered that at this time the T & R section was effectively a separate part of the Society for the 'communicators' as opposed to the 'experimenters'.

It consisted of a two-valve arrangement which employed a choke-modulated oscillator for transmission. The same valves were changed to a detector and low-frequency amplifier configuration for reception by means of a four-pole two-position switch. This was of the so-called 'low-capacity' type which provided break-before-make. This was essential since the switch-

ing was arranged so as to change over the grids and anodes of both valves which were operating at different voltages, to suit the two different conditions of operation.

As can be seen from the circuit diagram on page 43, the heart of the unit was the inductance. This had two separate parts - one for the transmitter, with an adjust-

The transceiver, above, which was described in *Wireless World*, August, 1926 and on the right its internals.

The cover of the first editon of the T & R Bulletin, otherwise known as the *Bull*.

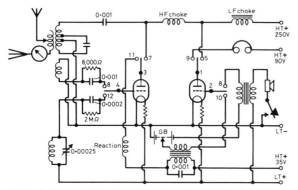

A circuit diagram of the transceiver described in *Wireless World*.

able grid coupling coil and, for receiving, a tuned coil with an adjustable reaction coil. Both of these were intended to be set to the best position but were not continuously adjustable.

The operating wavelength was 90 metres. Valves were specified as DE5/5A for the oscillator/detector and modulator/amplifier respectively, or an LS5/5A combination could be used for higher power.

Note that the unit was operated with an old GPO 'candlestick' telephone microphone and receiver.

Incidentally, Haynes later became editor of *Wireless World*.

Chapter 5

Some Notable Stations (1927 – 1933)

F R Neill, G5NJ

Here we see an unusual method of assembly in which most of the individual components are tidily fixed to the wall. The power valve can be seen at the top centre of the picture and would appear to be one of the DET2 150 watt dull-emitter valves, which were not often seen in amateur stations.

F R Neill 5NJ, Co. Antrim, Ireland, cc 1928.

✧ ✧ ✧

J W Mathews, G6LL

James Mathews was one of the early experimenters who followed up the first successful 200 metre transatlantic transmissions a year or two later. Although very active in Society affairs he is probably best remembered as the first British station to make contact with America on 10 metres. The transmitter he used for this was a classic example of the then state of the art. It comprised a straightforward crystal oscillator followed by frequency doublers to reach the final frequency, and these drove a DET15W 50W dull-emitter triode. The transmitter and circuit is shown below. Another photograph shows Mathews adjusting his 1933-vintage 20/40 metre transmitter. The typical

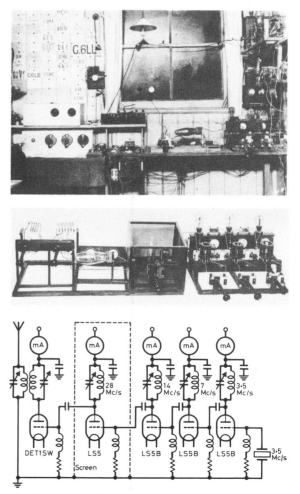

The 10 metre transmitter together with a circuit diagram.

constructional techniques of the period are clearly shown. The output stage uses a T250 valve, which is visible below the coil; below this is a frequency doubler and near the bottom is a DE5B crystal oscillator.

J W Mathews 6LL, with his 1933 transmitter.

✧ ✧ ✧

B Clapp, G2KZ

Ben Clapp was originally licensed before the war and received his new callsign shortly afterwards. He soon became interested in the possibility of long-range television transmission using the Baird system and proposed a transatlantic test. A licence for the unusually high power of 2 kW was obtained. The transmitter and its circuit is shown in the next column.

It consisted of a standard amplitude-modulated power amplifier using a fan-cooled silica triode in the output stage, which is seen in the picture just in front of Clapp on the right. The two large glass valves in front of the seated John Logie Baird were the modulator stage. The high-voltage power supplies were obtained from generators driven by a 9 hp motor and

giving 2 kV and 4 kV. The aerial was a 65ft-long five-wire cage of 18 inches diameter some 50ft high, which had a ten- wire counterpoise; the operating frequency was 45 metres.

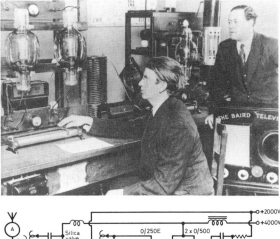

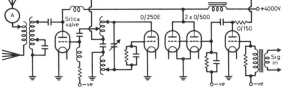

First transatlatic television from station 2KZ using the Baird system. The picture shows John L Baird (seated) with Ben Clapp 2KZ. Below the picture is a circuit diagram of 2KZ.

In 1927 Clapp visited the USA in order to set up a receiver at the station of W2CVJ while friends made test transmissions from G2KZ. On 8 February 1928 the first television transmission took place.

✧ ✧ ✧

H E Whatley, G2BY

In contrast to some of the high-power stations illustrated elsewhere in this book, many members were using typical low-power stations such as that shown on the next page.

This was owned by H E Whatley, G2BY, of Hammersmith and used a TPTG transmitter with a DE5. Its input was 7-8W delivered by a rotary converter supplied from a 12V accumulator. The aerial was an end-fed Hertz and the receiver was an 0-V-2 with reacting detector and two-valve LF amplifier. Note the Amplion loudspeaker.

45 Metre Transmitter G2DX, c.1926

The station of G E Whatley G2BY, 1929.

Some Early QSL Cards

❖ ❖ ❖

J D Chisholme, G2CX

'Chis' was one of the original *T & R Bulletin* editors, along with his close friends Jimmy Matthews, G6LL, and Geoff Thomas, G5YK. His activities were well-known in the late 'twenties and the picture shows his

transmitting equipment. This was typical of its time, being a simple open breadboard construction using a DE5B crystal oscillator, an LS5B doubler and a DET1 power amplifier. The 800V power supply with its two rectifier valves (together with warning notice) can be seen on the table below the transmitter, and a small TPTG 10 metre transmitter is also seen on the right. The aerial was a 66ft wire connected directly to the anode coil of the power amplifier - a practice which was subsequently forbidden in later licences!

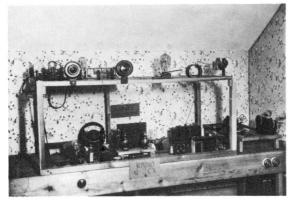

The station of J D Chisholme 2CX.

✧   ✧   ✧

F W Miles, G5ML

Miles first became interested in wireless in 1922 and soon obtained a transmitting licence. His first station was located in Beechwood Avenue, Coventry and his first transmitter - a TPTG - can be seen below.

The station of F W Miles G5ML.

With this he experimented on 10 metres and made regular contacts with ZS4M before progressing to a

RSGB and the Wireless League

APPROVED TRADER
OFFICIALLY APPOINTED
BY THE
(INC)
RADIO SOCIETY
OF
GREAT·BRITAIN
AND THE
WIRELESS LEAGUE

AND REPAIRER

By 1926 the business of servicing and repair of broadcast receivers was growing rapidly. The Wireless League, which was 'an organisation for the protection of the broadcast listener', was greatly concerned about standards and approached the RSGB to assist in a scheme to protect the rights of the broadcast listener.

A scheme of approval was duly arranged, and dealers accepted into the scheme were entitled to display the sign shown above.

The radio station for which F W Miles G5ML had primarily built his new house in 1930.

Sir Oliver Lodge

In 1925 Sir Oliver Lodge, who had been made an honorary member of the Society in 1914, became President. Lodge was a many-sided man; his research into radio waves and the behaviour of electrons had brought him a knighthood but he was also interested in theories of consciousness and had become convinced of the survival of life after death. In his book **Raymond** *he wrote eloquently of communication through mediums with the spirit of his son who had been killed in battle in World War 1. More prosaically, he was the first to describe the mechanism of 'secondary emission' and explain its effect on the characteristics of a tetrode - an effect which is still relevant to users of the famous 4CX250 family of valves today.*

Another 1925-vintage station is shown above. This was G5DC, of which the licensee was W. T. Aked; it is an attractive and compact station which was active on both CW and telephony. The transmitter was either a master oscillator/ amplifier arrangement or, more likely, a self-oscillator with the second valve acting as an

'absorber' - a method used extensively by commercial and ship stations.

Judging by its controls the receiver is a simple two-valve 0-V-1. The tuning controls are GEC slow-motion drive condensers, which were popular at the time.

In passing, it's worth mentioning that early Mullard transmitting valves can be identified by the large exhaust tube protruding from the top of the valve. Marconi and Osram valves had only a small side seal-off pip, and Mullard valves later adopted this form.

more powerful transmitter with 'Goyder lock' frequency control of its 50W output stage using a DET1.

In 1930, however, he was able to move to a new house at Gibbet Hill, Kenilworth, which he had built primarily for the radio station shown on the preceding page.

Note the powerful glow from inside the cabinet on the left of this picture! The top half of the cabinet housed a 40 metre transmitter using a 3.5 MHz crystal oscillator and doubler. The circuit used a DET1 driving an MT9F with 2.5 kV on the anode. On 20 metres

the same oscillator/doubler combination was used to drive a pair of UV201As to drive the final amplifier, which used a pair of DET2s in push-pull. The main receiver, seen in the centre of the operating table, is an 0-V-1 with a 'screened grid' SG215 detector and a PT2 LF pentode amplifier. The use of a tetrode for the detector allowed smoother control of reaction than was available with ordinary triodes. The receiver on the right is an early superheterodyne.

G5ML was the first Empire Link station to be appointed by the Society; he also won the Marcuse

F C (Dud) Charman, BEM, G6CJ

In the mid-twenties, many authorities were sceptical of the existence of a reflective layer in the upper atmosphere which had been postulated by Kennelly and Heaviside. However, an experiment by Appleton and Barnet in 1925 using the BBC's long-wave transmitter gave evidence of reflection. In 1927 there was a total eclipse of the sun, with the shadow passing across Northern England. It occurred to Charman and H A M Clark, G6OT - who were both working in Bedford at the time - that this would be a good opportunity to attempt to measure the height of the reflective layer. They therefore arranged with G5YG of Glasgow to radiate a carrier on 160 metres for several days, including the day of the eclipse. A suitable receiver with two stages of neutralised HF amplifiers, giving enough output to operate a milliammeter (a rare thing in those days!) was available but some means of making a recording had to be devised. A record was made using a roll of paper tape about two inches wide, which was pulled by a small Meccano motor. The paper passed over a frame with a transverse narrow slot, so that the observer could follow the meter pointer; the timing at one-minute intervals was arranged to mark the paper by a foot pedal.

The signal from Glasgow was received on the days prior to the eclipse and was fairly consistent. When the eclipse took place, very good interference patterns were obtained at the beginning and end of the event, as shown in the reproduction on the right. Charman and Clark calculated that the height of the layer was 50 – 100 miles; greater accuracy would have been possible if better meteorological data had been available to the observers.

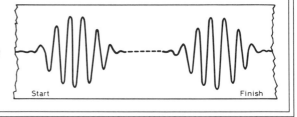

Start   Finish

ROTAB Cup and in 1932 the senior BERU contest. The aerials used were two Zepp-fed 67ft tops with 45ft feeders.

✦ ✦ ✦

S A French, G6FN, Edinburgh

In this station separate transmitters are available for the 28, 14, 7, 3.5 and 1.7 MHz bands. Each consists of a crystal oscillator and as many frequency doublers as required, using LS5B valves followed by amplifiers. On 28 MHz, however, a self-excited oscillator was used. The aerial system is a centre-fed 7 MHz half-wave with 65ft feeders. The receiver is a conventional 0-V-1 with a screened grid detector and a pentode LF amplifier.

The station of S A French G6FN.

Gerald Marcuse, G2NM

Nowadays the British Broadcasting Corporation's short-wave transmissions to the world in more than thirty languages from Bush House in London are taken for granted. However, the origin of short-wave broadcasting to overseas countries lies with Gerald Marcuse, the first honorary secretary of the T & R section of the RSGB. Marcuse first began his wireless experiments before World War 1 with a spark transmitter and crystal receiver; unfortunately no details of his equipment at that time are available but it must have been similar to that illustrated elsewhere in this book. He came into the Society as a result of its absorption of the Radio Transmitters Society, of which he had been honorary secretary. Marcuse became honorary secretary of the newly-formed T & R section and later took up the same post in the RSGB. It was in this capacity that he led the RSGB delegation to the Paris conference in 1925, when the International Amateur Radio Union was formed. He was elected President of the Society in 1929-30, and created an honorary member in 1946.

Marcuse was amongst the most active long-distance communicators of the day, and came to the notice of his contemporaries when he maintained contact with the Royal Geographical (sometimes referred to as the 'Rice-Henderson') Expedition to Brazil, for which purpose he obtained a high-power licence from the GPO.

Although much of his early work was done using CW, Marcuse soon became interested in the value of broadcasting speech and music overseas. He obtained a high-power licence in order to carry out experimental transmissions of speech and music items to the various countries

of the then Empire, and he was soon being heard all over the world on 32.5 metres.

After some two years the 'Empire broadcasting service' originated by G2NM was officially closed down and the BBC took over.

The picture in the previous column is the well-known one of Marcuse's station; it has been published many times and was reproduced on the front cover of the February 1988 edition of Radio Communication.

Less well-known, perhaps, is the picture above, which shows the same station from almost the same standpoint but in a rather different state. The beautiful superheterodyne receiver constructed for Marcuse by Alford, G2DX, is prominent in both pictures.

The following photographs show different aspects of G2NM, and the final picture shows the antenna he used for the broadcasts. Marcuse

continued on next page

continued from preceding page

was a colourful and creative character, and it is pleasant to be able to record that some of his equipment survives and is displayed at the Chalk Pits Museum, Amberley in Sussex.

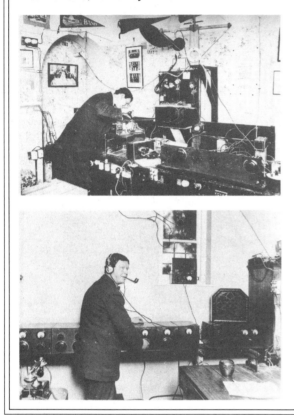

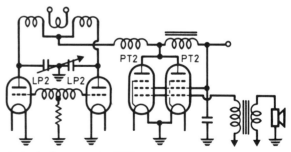

Five Metres in the Air

At the beginning of the thirties there were a number of stations active on the 5 metre band and it was becoming clear that propagation characteristics in this part of the spectrum were somewhat different from those of the short wave bands, being quasi- optical under normal conditions. It occurred to George Jessop, G6JP, and Douglas Walters, G5CV, that there might be a case for demonstrating the value of this wavelength for airborne operation as an alternative to the longer wavelengths currently being used by the Services.

It was fortunate that G6JP had access to a factory roof 80ft above the ground for the antenna, although this would involve a feeder length of some 175ft. Two sets of simple battery-operated equipment were constructed, the transmitter consisting of a push- pull pair of triode valves in a 'TNT' circuit modulated by a pair of audio pentodes in parallel. The receivers were Armstrong-type 'super-regens' using three valves each.

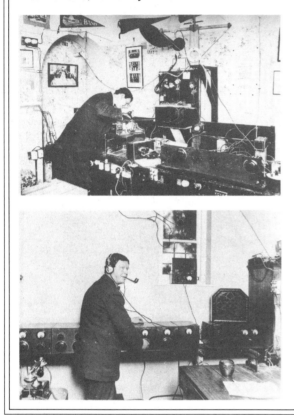

A circuit diagram of the 'TNT' transmitter.

In order to get transmitters and receivers on the correct wavelength a simple wavemeter was con-

5TH. ANNUAL CONVENTION 1930

ST. JAMES'S PALACE,
S.W.1.

11th May 1934.

On the occasion of the 21st anniversary of the Radio Society of Great Britain it affords me great pleasure to offer you my sincere congratulations on the material assistance which has been afforded by the Society and its individual members in the development of wireless as we now know it.

Wireless telegraphy and broadcasting are outstanding achievements of the age and their rapid progress during the last decade would have been impossible without the enthusiasm and research of the amateurs, headed by the Radio Society of Great Britain.

Edward P

PATRON.

The letter reproduced above is self-explanatory; the Vandyk drawing on the right is of the Prince of Wales, who ascended the throne as King Edward VIII in January 1936.

structed, which was calibrated by means of Lecher lines about 35ft long. As a matter of fact (and hoping that the DTI will not prosecute retrospectively), it is not known whether the frequency used was in the allocated 5 metre band! However, the wavemeter was passed around a number of West London stations so that they could all get on similar frequencies and no complaints were ever received from the GPO . . . .

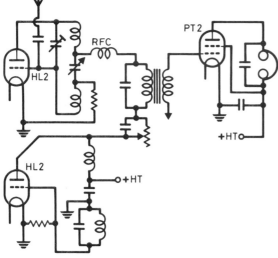

A circuit diagram of the Armstrong type Super Regen Receiver.

The aerial used was designed by George Exeter, G6YK. It consisted of a delta-matched half-wave

The simple wavemeter which G Jessop G6JP and D Walters G5CV constructed in order to get the transmitters and receivers onto the correct wavelength.

A Brown, G2BQ, Manchester

In this photograph the 'cabinet' form of transmitter is clearly seen, together with associated meters, etc.

dipole set up in an east-west direction. The feeder line was an open-wire arrangement consisting of 26 swg wire with ¼ inch wooden dowel spreaders which had

A picture of the 175ft feeder line up to the factory roof.

A E (Arthur) Watts, G6UN

Watts came to prominence in the Society with his design of a membership certificate, which was adopted and used for over thirty years. He was co-opted on to Council in 1929 and almost immediately became the 'father' of the recently-formed British Empire Radio Union. This was a world-wide section of the Society of which, thanks to the encouragement of Watts, most of the colonial societies became members.

Watts attended the 1932 Madrid International Telecommunications conference as an IARU observer

In 1934 he became President and served in this office for three years; in 1938 he was again elected President for a further three years and during this period he was involved in the Society's part of the formation of the Royal Air Force's Civilian Wireless Reserve (CWR). In 1938 he attended the Cairo International Telecommunications conference on the Society's behalf.

As President he was 'persona grata' at the Post, Foreign and Colonial Offices, and his proposed callsign series for the 'VP' colonies was welcomed and adopted by the Colonial Office.

A picture of the original 56MHz aerial 80ft above the ground.

been previously boiled in paraffin wax (in parenthesis, this feeder system survived for many years with no failures in spite of continual chafing against an adjacent wall). We did not know how much power was radiated, but since the transmitter was operated from a 120V battery it can only have been of the order of milliwatts. Indeed, in the course of initial tests between Hammersmith and Bedford Park in Chiswick, about a mile and a half away, satisfactory contact was maintained with an HT of only 9V from a grid bias battery!

One obvious difficulty was that in order to conduct tests with an aircraft, someone would have to pay for the hire of the machine(s) and pilot. Fortunately, at that time G5CV was Radio Correspondent of the *Daily Herald* and he managed to persuade them to sponsor the initial experiment, which was for G5CV to fly from Heston Aerodrome in an easterly direction over Essex and the North Sea. Results of the first test were very encouraging, although two-way contact could not take place because G6JP's receiver had been taken in the aircraft as a spare in case of failure.

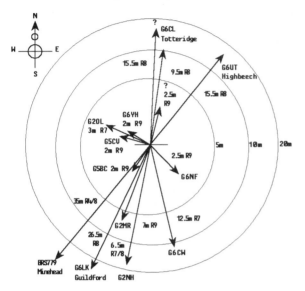

A plot of the signals received at Hammersmith.

The next experiment involved two de Havilland Dragon Moth aircraft, and the hire costs were shared by the *Daily Herald* and *Popular Wireless* magazine; G6JP was in the aircraft hired by the latter. The airborne aerials consisted of simple dipoles made from standard lighting flex. Trailing long wires were also available but in the event they were not used. Passenger seats were removed and the operators and observers sat on the floor.

On the day scheduled for the tests the weather was very bad, so much so that the pilot would not get airborne until there was some improvement. During the enforced delay the local Marconi man arrived at Romford and promptly refused permission for the aircraft to take off on the grounds that he had not approved the aerials and equipment. After some lengthy argument, during which the weather was clearing, he was locked in his hut whilst the aircraft took off!

Very good air-air and air-ground communication was obtained during the lengthy flight. A report on the experiment was published on the front page of the *Daily Herald* and in that week's edition of *Popular*

Wireless. The July 1933 issue of the *T & R Bulletin* also carried an account of the tests.

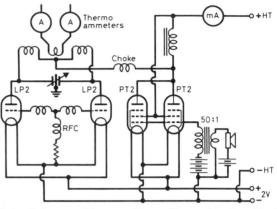

A circuit diagram of the ground transmitter used for the midget receiver.

In the following year attention was turned to the possibilities of communication with gliders. For this G6JP produced a midget receiver using HL2K and PT2K valves.

The receiver and batteries were fitted into a small case with aerial and phone leads coming out so that the

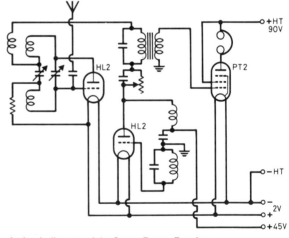

A circuit diagram of the Super-Regen Receiver.

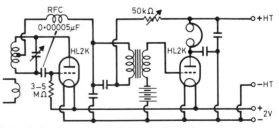

A circuit diagrams of the Self-quench Super Regen.

A typical Convention photograph, taken on the steps of the Institution of Electrical Engineers in the late 'thirties. The then President, A E Watts, G6UN, is at the front.

pilot could stow the case out of his way. In the course of the flight, instructions from the ground transmitter could be seen to be received, and on landing the pilot was most enthusiastic. A report appeared in the *T & R Bulletin* for October 1935. Just to round off the 5 metre story, tests were made from a station on the summit of Snowdon in August 1935. Signals were heard up to 180 miles away.

Chapter 6

The Society at War

When Hitler, despite assurances given a year earlier, launched his mighty war machine against Poland. He had already subdued Czechoslovakia and Austria, but Poland resisted. Great Britain had a Treaty with Poland, and honouring this, declared war on the Reich at 11 am on 3 September 1939. Signs of war had been building up for some years and by the time it came, the public had been prepared and plans were ready for rationing of food and all material supplies. However, if the Fuhrer had turned first on us the World would be very different today. In fact, he gave us a breathing space of a few months - the 'phoney war'.

This story is of how the Society and some of its members were affected and how it survived that war. To set the scene we must first explain the status of the Society at that time.

Up to 1939 about 4000 Amateur Licences had been issued, including G2, 3, 5, 6 and 8, plus a few 4s + all two letters except a couple of hundred 2 + three letter artificial aerial licensees. The Society membership was about 3000, including a number of overseas members.

In 1932, after some years of voluntary service in various offices, John Clarricoats, G6CL, was contracted as Secretary and installed in the office at 53 Victoria Street, London, together with his assistant May Gadsden. This was the start of a great career which was going to affect Amateur Radio throughout the whole world; he was once described as a 'human powerhouse'.

In 1932 there was an approach to the armed services to develop volunteer reserves of amateurs. The Royal Navy responded quickly and the Royal Naval Wireless Auxillary Reserve was formed; The Royal Air Force finally responded in 1938 with its Civilian Wireless Reserve (CWR); the Army had not when war came (see RSS later).

Formation of Civilian Wireless Reserve of the RAF

During the Society's Convention in September 1938, at the invitation of Council, Air Commodore C W Nutting, Director of signals RAF, who incidentally had met Paul Godley at the time of the Transatlantic tests, addressed the meeting on the proposal to form a Civilian Wireless Reserve. He outlined in detail the Air Ministry's proposals and this was well received by the majority of those present.

There were, however, one or two members who voiced their objection to the militarisation of amateurs. The President, Arthur Watts, G6UN, was very incensed at these objectors, so much so that he took the unusual step of leaving the chair on the rostrum and walked round the floor saying "Now I am one of you", and proceeded to say what he thought of the few objectors. Following this it was wholeheartedly approved by the members present.

This matter was regarded as of considerable importance and the text of the address was included in the September issue of the T&R Bulletin for the benefit of those present at the meeting.

There was a considerable response to the call to this service. All those who enlisted became members of the R A F V R, many of whom were to distinguish themselves on active service later.

The services benefited enormously from having amateurs readily available either trained or well skilled in radio.

The *T & R Bulletin* which had started in 1925, was by 1939 running to over 700 pages per annum. However, until then the only comprehensive manual of Amateur Radio was the *ARRL Handbook* which was imported and sold by the Society. In 1933 a small booklet was produced - the Guide to Amateur Radio. Written by T. Palmer Allan, GI6YW, it was to encourage the uninitiated into the fold. Year by year, especially at the annual Radio Show, it sold in thousands and by 1938 it had grown to 60 pages, as large as the monthly *Bull*. It was then that Council decided to produce a full scale manual with a target size of 220 pages. Starting with the Guide, experts in their various subjects sweated away under the lash of Jack Clarricoats and the eye of the Technical Committee, and in December 1938 the 280 page *Amateur Radio Handbook* was launched. It was a bold venture of uncertain outcome, but at a price of Two Shillings and Sixpence (12.5p)* it was tremendous bargain. The whole printing of 5000 copies was sold out in a few weeks. So a second printing of 3000 was ordered. These were delivered the day before war was declared!

The badge of RAFCWR as published in November 1938 issue of the *T & R Bulletin*.

Financially, the balance sheet for the year ending 30 September showed a turnover of £2,800 of which £1,000 was salaries, and £1,160 the cost of the *Bull*.

---

*   To bring this price into perspective it should be noted that at that time £5 per week would have been a very good wage for a skilled technician.

Running costs accounted for the rest. Members subscriptions did not cover the total, but sales of publications just topped them up to leave a profit of a few pounds, a figure which would be described scientifically as 'within the limits of experimental error'! There was, however, a reserve fund of about £1,400.

This then is the background against which the President, Arthur Watts, G6UN, called an emergency meeting of the Council one week after the outbreak of war. The Secretary and nine of the possible twelve officers and Council were present.

There was no doubt about a determination to 'carry on', but the problem facing them was not whether, but how? Many of the factors affecting a decision were at least uncertain and some unknown. With the reservists disappearing into uniform in hundreds, would the income get too small? Could the Bulletin continue? And what about those 3000 new handbooks? And so on.

'Clarry' pushed the boat out with a noble offer to work from home in Southgate and carry on as long as possible. It was decided to keep the office at number 53 as a postal address and store, and reduce the staff from five to two. (The office was abandoned in late 1940 after Bomb damage).

The London area subscription was reduced to 15 shillings in line with the rest of the UK and to 10 shillings for those on active service. The Bulletin would continue in reduced size and our advertisers had already promised continued support to continue the policy of good technical articles and to encourage members to continue with experimental work as far as possible.

Council proceedings were not normally published in those days, but it was decided to circulate the membership by post with these decisions.

The August 1939 Bulletin showed little sign of the coming war. The September issue, as normal, would have appeared on the 15th, and much of it must have already been ready for the printers. When it appeared, probably rather late, it was already a wartime issue! One can imagine the tremendous effort by the office, and probably the printer too, to do this. The new editorial by the President records the decisions of the special meeting. The famous notice in the London Gazette by the Postmaster General, terminating all licences for experimental Wireless Telegraphy, was included.

Some of the regular items had to be changed, and many of the advertisers had re-made their entries. As a result of the circular letter there were quotations of congratulations received from the members. There

Numb. 34661   5973

SUPPLEMENT

TO

The London Gazette

Of TUESDAY, the 29th of AUGUST, 1939

Published by Authority

Registered as a newspaper

THURSDAY, 31 AUGUST, 1939

WIRELESS TELEGRAPHY ACTS,
1904 TO 1926.

To ALL HOLDERS OF LICENCES FOR EXPERI-
MENTAL WIRELESS TELEGRAPH TRANSMITTING
STATIONS.

I, Major The Right Honourable George
Clement Tryon His Majesty's Postmaster
General hereby give notice that in pursuance
of the provisions therein contained all licences
for the establishment of wireless telegraph
sending and receiving stations for experimental
purposes are hereby withdrawn.

Dated this thirty-first day of August 1939.

G. C. Tryon,

His Majesty's Postmaster General.

N.B.—This Notice has no application to the
ordinary wireless receiving licences issued to
the general public at Post Offices throughout
the country.

WIRELESS TELEGRAPHY ACTS,
1904 TO 1926.

To ALL HOLDERS OF LICENCES FOR EXPERI-
MENTAL WIRELESS TELEGRAPH TRANSMITTING
STATIONS.

I, Major The Right Honourable George
Clement Tryon His Majesty's Postmaster
General hereby give notice that in pursuance
of the provisions therein contained all licences
to establish wireless telegraph receiving stations
for experimental purposes and to use wireless
sending apparatus in conjunction with "artificial" aerials are hereby withdrawn.

Dated this thirty-first day of August 1939.

G. C. Tryon,

His Majesty's Postmaster General.

N.B.—This Notice has no application to the
ordinary wireless receiving licences issued to
the general public at Post Offices throughout
the country.

The famous notice in the London Gazette by the Postmaster General, terminating all licences for experimental wireless.

War Time Membership.

During the war an economy membership certificate/membership card was issued, being 6.5 by 5 inches, in lightweight card folded in the middle to form the membership card, both sides of this are illustrated.

was a SOS from the War Office begging amateurs to join the Royal Signals and the front cover was filled with a notice from the Press Association exhorting all manufacturers to continue advertising. Finally, since Douglas Chisholm, G2CX, who ran the QSL Bureau, had been 'called up' into service, there was a notice advising members to send all QSL Cards and associated correspondence to Arthur Milne, G2MI, a service which he continued for the rest of his working life!

The October edition was reduced from the usual 60 to 30 pages. Arthur Milne's *Month on the Air* was changed to *Month off the Air*. New regular pages had been introduced - *On Active Service*, a list of about 50 members already called up; (over a page full in November). Another regular *Khaki and Blue* gave news to and from the 'boys' in active service. There was also the first Silent Key notice, Jack Hamilton, G5JH, lost with HMS Courageous.

And so went the RSGB to war, with the *Bull* thin at times, but never missing publication, and in spite of the slings and arrows of the enemy, keeping in touch with the lads away from home and always providing a technical article of some sort. In spite of strict rationing, the Secretary was able to persuade the Paper Controller that the RSGB was an effective part of the war effort, and paper was provided for the Society's publications, then and throughout the war.

It is not the purpose here to continue the war story, but one thing must be mentioned; namely how the Handbook became an all-time best seller and saved the Society. The second printing was sold out in weeks! Orders were still pouring in. It had become a technical manual for the Services!

A second edition, price three shillings and sixpence (17.5p) was prepared with an extra chapter on Television; very useful for anybody concerned with Radar or other things using cathode ray tubes or pulsology. It was published in August 1940, and a note in the December *Bull* said 'hurry up; we have only 30 copies left'! And so it continued throughout the war, to a total of over 180,000 copies and 100,000 copies of a supplementary book. It was said that this, on one set of typeface, was an all-time record. By 1946-7 the Society had over 13,000 members and nearly £1 per member in the reserve fund.

Dud Charman, G6CJ, was involved in some of the episodes given in this story, but memory is fickle, and much reference was made in the Bulletins of those days. In particular, also reference must be acknowledged to John Clarricoats' classic book *The World at Their Fingertips*, for checking dates and figures.

The Radio Security Service

Apart from the way in which the Society 'did its bit' during the war, there was another service by Radio Amateurs and others which turned out to be an important contribution to the war effort: the work of the

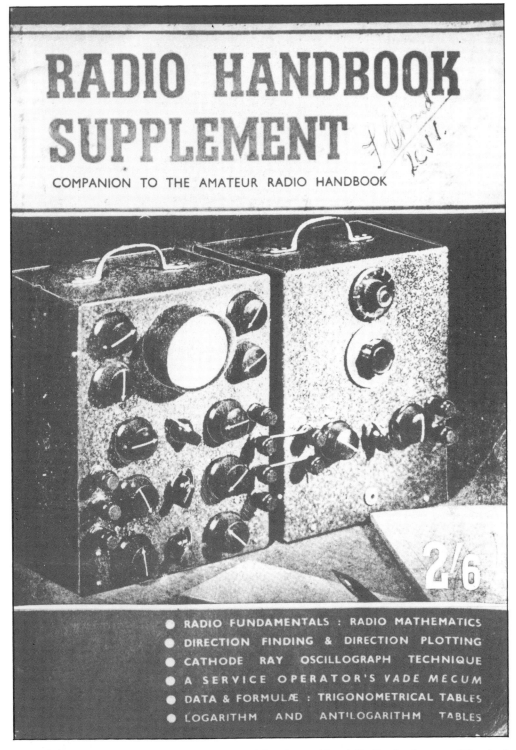

The Amateur Radio Handbook (left) and The Radio Handbook Supplement (above). The Handbook was an all-time best seller and became a technical manual for the Services.

Voluntary Interceptors (V.I.s) of the Radio Security Service (R.S.S.) in monitoring the shortwave radio spectrum.

This was carried out under such strict security that even when the war was over, it was many years before some of the story could be made public. The V.I.s were committed to secrecy for life. However, after a long period gaining clearance from the Ministry of Defence, Paul Wright of the B.B.C. was able to present the documentary television programme "The Secret Listeners" in 1979. Later Nigel West was able to publish his book *G.C.H.Q.* in 1987. This latter contains a whole chapter devoted to R.S.S. of considerable interest to the V.I.s who had never been able to know the results of their efforts. Here is a record as seen from V.I. level, below, of the way the radio amateur played his part.

Radio monitoring had been in operation from the time of the 1914 war, at which time amateurs were considered quite unsuitable for the work! Little did they know! By 1939 there were a number of civilian volunteers, working in secret for the R.S.S., such as retired seagoing operators, but the whole intelligence gathering system was quite inadequate for war when it loomed up in 1938-9 and it was necessary to expand the service. The radio monitoring task was given to Lord Sandhurst, who had in fact been a radio amateur. He went to the Society to meet the President, Arthur Watts, G6UN, to see if they could help.

Arthur Watts was a city merchant, who had for some time worked in the Admiralty Room 40 and understood exactly what was needed. Yes: R.S.G.B. could certainly help. They had many hundreds of members (wither) retired or in essential jobs, not likely to be called up, who knew all about fishing for rare signals under an overlay of noises various: that is what amateur radio is all about.

The entire Council of the Society was nominated as a start, followed later by Society representatives in the various regions of the UK, as possible leaders of the groups to be formed. It has been stated that at the end of 1939 there were only seven Voluntary Interceptors at work in the London area, but it must be remembered that it was necessary to obtain security clearance before a potential V.I. could be approached.

G6CJ was enrolled at Christmas 1939 and soon after attended a meeting with Arthur Watts, Major Sandhurst, Capt. Sabine, (R.Sigs.) and three others. The four (G6NF, G6CJ, G6OT, G2CD) were to become Group Leaders for the sectors around London, and a scheme was worked out for sharing the work between the groups, under Sabine, as the Regional Officer Home South. Arthur Watts then toured the Country and within a few months there were 400 V.I.s at work.

There was an advantage in having the receiving stations well spread, because radio propagation is fickle, and at times what would be heard in London might be very different from what could be picked up in Scotland or even the West. It was expected that if an enemy agent started up anywhere in this country there would be a V.I. near enough to recognise from experience that it was a local suspect station. They were also instructed to concentrate on a given slice of the spectrum, learn to recognise all the regular users, and our own fighting services, but report anything unusual or irregular.

Radiotelegraphy is for exchanging messages. In order to do this the operators must have regular times, frequencies, and link up according to schedule; even if they have no traffic they have to keep their channel open. They use regular procedures and codes for linking up, dealing with interference and poor signal conditions, correcting errors and so on. In regular communication this is done by means of internationally agreed codes and procedures. A normal method of calling up, for example, might be as "ABC de DEF" and those calls would identify the two stations.

The fighting services each have their own systems which are quite distinctive but not basically secret, though messages might be encoded. In the case of clandestine operations, attempts are made at concealment. They might try to imitate a regular system, or use secret procedures which would immediately mark them as suspect. In any case, if they get into difficulties and revert to plain language they give away information leading toward their identification, or helping in the decipherment of the message.

What did the V.I.s find? Well, there was not much heard about local agents, though even if the V.I. had found something, he would not have been told of the outcome. What they did find was a large number of suspect stations which they were encouraged to watch. Those who understood propagation soon came to know that these signals were coming in from all over Europe, and even on long haul circuits.

The V.I.s were required to include a note of one or two of the regular occupants of their band, useful as a frequency check, times of interception and on everything suspect, a complete record as accurately as possible of everything sent including comments, mistakes and back-chat - all useful information.

Logs were posted as soon as possible, and here a word of praise must be recorded for the work of the G.P.O., for the famous address 'Box 25 Barnet' to which logs were sent must have been recognised as something important and in reach of London logs posted as late as 3 am had a good chance of reaching 'BOX' in the first delivery. After posting the logs were sometimes returned with encouraging comments such as 'Suspect', 'More please' or 'Covered thanks' and advice to learners.

The suspect stations, of course, did their best to avoid interception; usually the other end of a coupled pair was on a different frequency; the callsigns might be changed daily on some sort of a rota, and in any case, only the one call would be used at each end, quite unusual and to the V.I. this was a help rather than a hinderance! Another typically teutonic trick was the use of 'QSA 0'. The QSA Code is a universal way of indicating quality of reception, with QSA5 for very good to QSA1 unreadable, but the zero when they couldn't make connection was unique - it had never been heard on the air before! In fact, amongst the ranks the R.S.S. was known as the 'QSA nought Club'. But apart from these aides there was always another factor. Every individual has his own 'fist', his way of sending the dots and dashes of morse code, and every transmitter has its own characteristic sound; they can be just as recognisable and different as human faces, hence a daily changing callsign was not a hindrance.

It was specialised knowledge such as this, common to amateurs and other radio operators, which made the V.I. so valuable. The mere knowledge of morse code is only the start.

It was not often that a V.I. could find the other one of a pair separated in frequency. First it requires two receivers and then even in a short space there might be hundreds of other signals between them. It was easier at 'BOX' because another log might bring in the missing link.

However, it was not all like that. The daily session for the average V.I. was just a monotonous 'grind', with only an occasional catch. Still, even so, they were a wonderful crowd and worked with a dedication that deserved the highest praise. And all they knew was that in some way they were making a contribution to victory.

There was the problem of the Military in charge of a civilian voluntary organisation. The different ways of thinking inevitably led to misunderstandings and frustrations, and the group leaders were in the middle. By the very nature of things instructions often had to be suddenly changed. They blamed the enemy and carried on.

To keep up the morale, for human or technical reasons, the group leaders often had to get round to their V.I.s, usually in the pitch dark with only a tin-hat for protection, and learning the way by a faint glimmer on the side of the road from what the wartime regulations had left of a headlamp. And ever the danger that the landscape might blow up in front of him. Occasionally there might be a local group - or regional meeting with somebody from Headquarters to tell them what was going on and leak a few well censored tales of their successes. These often took place in a free beer situation.

There were experts who needed no help: beginners to be educated: some were called up, some gave up. Some opted to join the Royal Signals and work in the special R.S.S. stations which had been built.

As time went on, new discoveries were taking their places - retired seagoing 'sparks' who fell in naturally, ex landline operators who were expert in morse (on a sounder) but knew nothing about how to find their way round on a radio receiver or how to extract weak signals from the 'noises off' and from the 'Hells Orchestra' of the radio jammers trying to prevent the broadcasting stations shouting war at each other.

Then there was always a receiver problem. There were never enough receivers. Amateurs could with the help of 'BOX' recover theirs which had been empounded by the G.P.O. at the outbreak of war. New intake often had no suitable receiver. Broadcast receivers with shortwave bands were converted. but their tuning arrangements were practically useless for this work. Headquarters were always promising, but could never find enough. At one stage it was said that a large consignment of HRO Receivers was on the way from the U.S.A., (the best of those times), but they were never seen; they were said to have been sunk. However, from information gathered many years later, it was not in the Atlantic; it was more likely they were diverted to another purpose. Such is the way in war.

Of course there was a security problem for the V.I. Everybody was doing his extra bit in some way or other. Neighbours wanted to know why they were not in the Home Guard, or in some other public effort like wardens of firewatching at night: their employers were suspicious. In difficult cases, like the one where a V.I. was marched off at revolver point because morse signals had been heard, 'BOX' could usually come to the rescue.

The problem was eventually solved by putting them

In the years when
Civilisation was menaced with destruction
F. J. H. Charman, B.E.M.,
who served 1939 ~ 1945
gave generously of his time, powers and
technical skill in essential service to his
Country.

Herbert Creedy

Telephones:
BARNET 6500 (4 Lines)
MILL HILL 4271 (4 Lines)

P.O. BOX 25
BARNET
HERTS.

It is with great pleasure that I forward
to you the attached certificate in recognition of the
valued and devoted service which you have voluntarily
rendered to our Organisation during the War.

This certificate is signed by Sir Herbert
Creedy who, during the War years when your work
was of the utmost value, was the head of the
Department to which we were responsible.

I would like to add my personal thanks
for all you have done and for the many hours of
hard work and personal self sacrifice you have
contributed.

Colonel,
Controller,
Radio Security Service.

The certificate (left) and the letter (above) which the Radio Security Service presented to Dud Charman G6CO, in recognition of the valuable service which he voluntarily gave to them during the war years.

into the uniform of a 'special branch' of the Royal Observer Corps. The uniform dispelled doubts, but sometimes raised a fresh problem. There might have been a local ROC post in the locality. And there were tales of V.I.s who had been feted by an aircraft crew which had been brought limping home to safety by the ROC; embarrassing to say the least. But the uniform would have considerably improved the V.I.s future if the enemy had ever invaded England.

And the result? By 1941 there were over 200 V.I.s in the London area alone. H.Q. was telling the V.I.s that although 'Jerry' was continually putting on new services, very few were ever missed. And later that our own agents out in Europe could send in their staff "blind" in the knowledge that it would surely get home. The result of the work of this organisation, the vase amount of information pouring in daily, which might never have been obtained in any other way, called for increased capacity at the intelligence centre, Bletchley Park. This information put together with that from other sources gave a knowledge of the enemy's plans and movements which was an essential contribution to final victory. This is a V.I.s story: the effect we had on other intercept organisations is more amply described in *GCHQ*. R.S.S. had stolen all the best interceptors.

For the epilogue. With the end of the war in Europe all our favourite suspects disappeared quite suddenly. The V.I.s were disbanded, and eventually received a letter of credit to hang on the wall. A number of King's medals were also distributed.

1. A typical suspect type of station (or FOX as we called them) was one which later achieved much Press publicity as 'The New York Spy'. One of the pre-war V.I.s, a retired ships operator, some months before the war had found him hiding in the 20-metre amateur band, sending coded messages. This stood out because amateurs were not permitted to do so.

   The station used a fixed callsign AOR and the messages were made up with the 'preamble' of groups of 4,4,3 and 3 letters, coding Date, Time, Serial number. and number. of letters, followed by text in 5-letter code groups. The agent was sending material of value to the enemy including information on shipping movements.

   Of course it was of great value to our intelligence to

know this. Also as it was so regular and typical it could be used for instructing new V.I.s. It vanished suddenly when U.S.A. entered the war in December 1941.

*"The King hath note of all
that they intend
By interception that they
dream not of"*

Henry V. Act II Scene II.

2. It was said, in due course, that due to the work of the R.S.S. we were able to keep a lead on the enemy, watching his network of spies growing, and that Hitler was never able to establish a system of agents in this country: they always met a reception committee. Here is a story of one such agent, sent over in advance of the planned invasion in 1941.

   He was forced to work for us, but after some time he would, if free, have run out of money, so a request was sent back to Germany. He was told to go to Victoria Station and get on a Nr. 11 Bus for Victoria. At the first stop a Japanese would get in next to him and get off at the next stop, leaving his newspaper behind. Then get off at stop three. One can wonder who else was on that bus, and what became of the son of heaven!

Arthur Watts, G6UN, H. M. Clark, G6OT and Dud Charman, G6CJ, were directly involved in this episode.

Appendix

The First Callbook ?

The following call sign pages are a faithful reproduction of the amended edition of Gamage's *Directory of Experimental Wireless Stations in the United Kingdom* which was published in March 1914, the first edition having been printed the previous year (July 1913).

At the time of publication of this book it is believed that there are now only two copies of the directory still in existence. This being the case, it is thought worthwhile recording Gamage's *Directory* in this book for posterity and many readers will, no doubt, gain much pleasure from browsing through the many fascinating entries from a bygone era.

Directory of Experimental Wireless Stations

Published by A. W. Gamage, March 1914

Official Call Letters	ADDRESS	NAME	Telephone No.	Power	Transmitting Wave Length (Meters)	Sending Range in Miles	Receiving Wave Length (Meters)	Receiving Range Miles	Remarks Transmitting	Usual Times of Working	Club of which a Member if any
A											
ABX	Highgate, 49, Claremont Road	F. Bennett		⅝ Coil	300		Any	1,000 Coil	Motor Cycle W. Assc.		
ACX	Moseley, Birmingham, "Homeleigh," Anderton Park Road	A. G. Cocks		Accum. 10 Watts	100	8	800	250		7–11 p.m.	B'ham
AGX	Forest Gate, 41, Claremont Road	T. W. Atkin		10 Watts	200	1	200 up			6–10 p.m.	
ALX	Middlesboro, 173, Newport Road	J. C. Appleton		80 Watts	200						
AVX	Braintree, Essex, London Road	H. N. Dyer		¼ Kw. Dynamo Accum.	300						
AXF	Grantham, Mowbray House	James W. Armstrong		50 Watts							
AXJ	Eltham, Kent, 12, Westmount Road	Capt. G. Maunde-Thompson, R.A.		50 Watts	200					6–10 p.m.	
AXL	Reading, 28, Castle Street	E. A. Tunbridge		50 Watts	200						
B											
BAX	Croydon, 6, The Waldrons	Model Engineer		50 Watts	300–600		450			2–5 p.m. & 8.30 p.m.–12	
BBX	King's Norton, Birmingham, "Fellbrigg," 95, Middleton Hall Road	Charles H. Bach		Accum. 20 Watts	150		100 to 4,000		1 in. Coil		B'ham Wireless
BGX	Oldham, West View, Rochdale Road	Cyril Buckley	160a	Batteries 50 Watts	200		200 upwards			8–12 p.m.	
BHX	Newport, (Mon) Bassaleg Road	C. H. Bailey		6 in. Coil							
BIX	Hove, Sussex, 4, Palmeira Avenue	George H. Bechtel	8884 Hove	Accum.	260	20	Any	1,000	Musical spark	8.15 p.m.	Derby Wireless
BJX	Redhill, Station Road	L. A. Brown		20 Watts	200	4				8.30 p.m.	
BOX	Richmond, 10, Onslow Road	G. G. Blake			300–600						
BQX	Blackburn, Simmons Street	Mr. Burton			250						
BVX	Blackpool, 92, Warley Road	J. F. Fish		Accum. 30 Watts	100	18	250	1,000		Evening	
BWX	Manor Park, 122, Byron Avenue	B. G. Watts									
BXI	Nottingham, Gordon L. Ruddington	L. M. Baker	28 Rud-ding't'n		200	30	up to 8,000	500	4 in. Coil	6.30–9 p.m.	Derby W'less Hon. Treas.
BXJ	Derby, Littleover Hill	W. Bemrose	105 Derby	Alt. ¼ Kw.	200	40	up to 8,000	1,500	Musical note and ordinary	Sundays, eves. by arrangm'nt.	Derby W'less Hon. Treas.
BXK	Warwickshire, Solihull, Berryfield	P. Stanley Beaufort	48 Solih'l	Accum.	Variable					Evenings	B'ham Wireless Assoc'n Treas.
BXM	Leeds, 4, Warwick Place	A. M. Bage			500	5	up to 5,000				

B—continued

Official Call Letters	NAME	ADDRESS	Telephone No.	Power	Transmitting Wave Length (Meters)	Sending Range in Miles	Receiving Wave Length (Meters)	Receiving Range Miles	Remarks Transmitting	Usual Times of Working	Club of which a Member if any
BXT	G. P. Bailey	Armswell, Wolvey, Nr. Hinckley		Accum.	Not yet complete		300–600	800		Morning and Evening	Derby Wireless
BXV	W. G. Bayman	Norbury, 7, Strathyre Avenue		Accum. 30 Watts	not over 200	2		1,000	1 in. Coil	7.30–10 p.m.	
BXZ	T. Brook	Huddersfield, 11, South Parade									
C											
CDX	R. W. Cox	Bristol, 16, Edgeumbe Road, Redland	2617X	24 Watts	200	10–12					Bristol W. Assoc.
CJX	C. A. Collins	Purley, Collinwood, Purley Knoll	39 Purley Joint Licence	Batteries 120 Watts	300	15	Std. Bi. 600	1,000	Syntonic	After 8 p.m.	Purley Cadio C.
CLB	Rev. K. Moillut	Harrogate, 78, Hgh Street, Starbeck		15 Watts	100	5	Any	600			
CLB	F. Pretty	Harrogate, Doric Lodge, Hookstone Lodge		15 Watts	100	5	Any	600			
CNX	J. Coxon	New Malden		Accum.	450						
CUX	F. China	Wandsworth, 24, Santos Road, West Hill		50 Watts	300	12	up to 10,000	800	Ordinary and Musical Notes	8–12 p.m.	
CVX	R. Chimes	Hove, Holmcroft, Wilbury Villas	2171X	12 Watts	400	2	200–5,000	700		7.30–10 p.m.	
CWX	A. H. Charters	Welling, Kent, 26, Granville Road			150						
CXC	P. W. Cuncliffe	Clitheroe (Lancs.), 8, market Place			300						
CXD	J. E. Catt	London, 20, Senegal Road, S.E.			150						
CXF	Portable Field Sets	Barnes, Wandsworth Common, etc.		10 Watts		5	up to 10,000		Only used occasionally		
CXG	P. Cockroft	Leeds, Elmhurst, Beeston		Accum.	500	8–12					
CXI	Corry	Anerley, 4, Weighton Road		100 Watts	250	10			8.30 p.m.		
CXJ	D. M. Cassidy	Westgate-on-Sea, Kent, St. James Vicarage		15 Watts	250	5–8	200–6,000	500–1,000	2–4 p.m. & 11.30 p.m.		
CXM	Manchester Educ. Com.	Fallowfield, Moseley Road, C. School		Accum.	150	20	100 up	1,000	4½ in. Coil High note	Sat. afternoon Sunday morn. Evening 7–11	London Wireless
CXO	A. H. Charters	Welling, Kent, 26, Granville Road		25 Watts	200	10				Evenings	
CXP	A. W. Chandler	Brighton, Chiswick Lodge, Tivoli Cres.		Accum. 50 Watts	200		up to 5,000	1,000		Evenings	
CXS	J. S. Chapman	Cricklewood, 114, Ivy Road		15 Watts	200	5	Any				
CXX	F. C. Stimson	Leyton, 57, Wesley Road		30 Watts	350						
CXZ	Fredk. Crompton	Bjury, 1, Warth Road		Storage Batt. 50 Watts	200	15	200–4,000	1,000	6 in. Spark Coil	Evening	M'ch'st'r Wireless
D											
DAX	Stanley Deakin	Old Southgate, N., "Salcombe" Avenue Road		Accum.	200	5	up to 2,500	300		8–10 p.m.	
DHX	P. Denison	Halifax, King's Cross, Wainhouse Tower		Mains 230 V 20 A	150–1,200		150–9,000	2,500	High musical note, var.	10–12 p.m. Sat. 3.15 p.m.	
DKX	M. de Aula Donnisthorpe	58, Kensington Mansions, S.W.									

Official Call Letters	NAME	ADDRESS	Telephone No.	Power	Transmitting Wave Length (Meters)	Sending Range in Miles	Receiving Wave Length (Meters)	Receiving Range Miles	Remarks Transmitting	Usual Times of Working	Club of which a Member if any
D—*continued*											
DMX	F. G. Marshall	Colchester		¼ K.w.	450						
DNX	Col. Dennis	Woolwich Arsenal		¼ K.w.	430						
DPX	Geo. Sharp	Durdham Down			200 Var.						
DSX	P. Denison	Halifax, Rostellon, Savile Park	1244	½ K.W. 16 Watts	150		150-2000	600	Poulsen Arc & ½ in. coil	10–12 p.m.	
DTJ	D. Roberts	Liscard, Cheshire, 11, Denton Drive									
DTX	A. Dinsdale	Glasgow, Strathmore, Airlie Drive, Mount Florida		250V'ts D.C. Main 50 Watts	200	50–80	250–8,500	1,500	6 in. Coil, Musical Note	Evenings	
DWX	B. J. Davies	Corra Linn, Cockshot Road, Reigate, Surrey		8 Volts Amp. Accum.	10–350	10	350	1,500	Ordinary 1 in. spark Coil and accessories	8–12 p.m.	
DXA	J. E. Dyer	Colchester, 215, Maldon Road		Ac. 48 Watts	200	15	10,000			6–12 p.m.	
DXB	A. C. Dufort	Putney, London, S.W., 25, Hazlewell Rd.		Stationary	200		100 up			After 6 p.m.	
DXD	A. V. Dodderidge	Dorchester, Commercial School		40 Watts Accum.	Set		300				
DXF	Joseph F. P. Deller	Battersea, London, S.W., 92, Chatham Road		Stationary	300	5		200	Ignition coil used.	9–11 p.m.	
DXE	A. V. Dodderidge	Dorchester, Commercial School		Acc. & Dyn.	Set		100 up	100			
DXJ	A. J. Dixon	Enfield, 1, Bedfords Villa, Southbury Road		20 Watts Accum.	200	8	300			After 6 p.m.	
DXN	Frank L. W. Dean	Worcester Park, Surrey, 71, Washington Road		10 Watts	200	8	100–4000	500	Auto-jigger	10.30–11a.m. 9–11 p.m. Sunday	
DXS	R. F. L. Dickey	Londonderry, 7, McCrea Magee College	348	Batt. dyna. 50 Watts	200	80	200	600–1,000		6–12 p.m. midnight	Liv'rpool A.W.A.
DXT	R. F. L. Dickey	Londonderry, 7, McCrea Magee College		Batteries	200	20	200		Portable Set	Sat. to Mon. & evenings	
DXW	R. durrant	Cricklewood, N.W. London, 121, Broadway	4101 HMP	Accum.	200	5	up to 6,000	1,000		8–11 p.m. Sundays 11–1 p.m. 8–11 p.m. Week days	
DXX	N. Driver	Bristol, Bishopaton, 13, Claremont Road									
DZX	J. W. Downes	Derby, 61, Arthur Street			200	10	8,000	1,000		After 6 p.m.	
E											
EMX	T. H. Schroeder	London, W., Redbourne Hotel, Great Portland Street		80 Watts	150						
ENX	H. F. Brand	London, Westminster City School, Palace Street		100 Watts	150–200						London Wireless
EOX	E. M. Eadie	Ayshire, West Kilbride, Langmuir	26	Accum. 30 Watts	200	20	up to 4,000	1,000		Week end	
ETX	A. Barber	Bradford, 15, Hartlington Terrace, Lidget Green		100 Watts	300						
EXB	A. J. Evans	Small Heath, Birmingham, Hugh Villas, Hugh Road		50 Watts Accum.	200	15	200 upwards.		2 in. coil Dipper break jigger		B'ham W. Ass.

Official Call Letters.	ADDRESS	NAME	Telephone No.	Power	Transmitting Wave Length (Meters)	Sending Range in Miles	Receiving Wave Length (Meters)	Receiving Range Miles	Remarks Transmitting	Usual Times of Working	Club of which a Member if any
E—*continued*											
EXC	Spennymoor, 7, Beaumont Terrace	F. A. Elliff		Ac. 45 Watts	200	5	200 up	1,000		8.30–11.30 p.m.	
EXD	Cricklewood, London, N.W., 6, Crickle Road	L. P. Elmer		40 Watts	200	10	up to 4,000	400		7–10 p.m. Sat. 3–10p.m.	London Wireless
EXG	Lyndhurst, Hants, St. Amands, forest Gardens	G. E. Eyston	17 Lynd hurst	Ac. 50 Watts	200		up to 6,000	700		Sat. nights and Sundays	
EXT	Manchester, "Thornlea," Edge Lane, Chorlton-cum-Hardy	h. J. Knudson		50 Watts	200		200 up			Evenings	Radio Scientific
F											
FEX	Derby, Derby School	Derby School	235	Dyna. & dry cells, 100 W.	200–600	20	Up to 14,000	2,500	1 in Coil	4.30–6 p.m. 8.30–9 p.m.	
FFX	Brighouse, Yorks., Spring Villa	P. Farren	23 X Hop 757	100 Watts	600	15	up to 7,000	2,000		7–11 p.m.	
FKX	London, S.E., Walcot House, Kennington Road	— Forman		S'cdny. Bat., 4 v. 10 amp.						8–12 p.m.	
FNX	Parsons Green, Fulham, 251, New Kings Road	G. H. Finlay	Putney 2094	Secondary Cells 10 Watts	100 (approx)	3–5	50–4,000	1,400	Tuning not very sharp	All Sunday, on and off, all week days	
FOX	Manningham, Bradford, 56 Oak Lane	W. S. Forman		Accum.	200	2	250–5,000	400			London Wireless
FPX	Sydenham, S.E., 53, Bishopsthorpe Road	F. Pinkerton		8–10 Volts 30 Accum.	150	15–20	100 up to 7,000	1,000	4 in. Coil 3 in. coil, high note, loose c'ple	8–10 p.m.	
FRX	Chiswick, 118, Cranbrook Road	F. O. Read									
FWX	London, W. Kensington, 52, Fairholme Road			100 Watts	100		100–1,600				
FXA	Croydon, 107, Park Lane	V. N. Fenton		Accum. 50 Watts	150	10	Any	400		6–10 p.m.	
FXG	Stockton-on-Tees, Ash Villa, Fairfield	C. G. Funnell		Mains	200						
FXK	Orford, Kent	S. H. Freeman		50 Watts Mains and Accum.	200				5 in. Coil		
FXN	Kenilworth, Stoneleigh Abbey Farm	L. G. Fish		20 Watts	200	10	200 up to	1,000		Evenings and week-ends	
FXQ	"Lisburn," Sevenoaks	Fulton (Major)	Svoaks. 202	200 Watts	450–750		250 upwards	1,000		Evenings after 6.30	
FXR	Birmingham, Midland Institute	Midland Institute		200							
G											
GBX	Banbury, Wood Green	J. A. Gillett	81 Ban- 179	20V. 5A.	400	10–20	300–6,000	1,000	Ord. and mus. note 15 words per minute.	Usual 10 a.m. to midnight.	
GFL	Longton, Staffs, 249, Florence Terrace, The Meir	F. Pamment	L'ngt'n	100 Watts	100		100–1,500	1,000			Stoke-on-Trent Wireless
GKX	Sussex, Orchard Leigh, Horeham Road	A. Goldsmith	378 Bexhill	50 Watts	200	25–30		1,000		After 8 p.m.	

G—continued

Official Call Letters.	ADDRESS	NAME	Telephone No.	Power	Transmitting Wave Length (Meters)	Sending Range in Miles	Receiving Wave Length (Meters)	Receiving Range Miles	Remarks Transmitting	Usual Times of Working	Club of which a Member if any
GLX	Lancashire, Roden, Langho	Harry Garstang	6 L'ho 175 Blckbn.	Primary 100 Watts		50		500		Week end and Evening	
GMA	Grantham, Mowbray House	J. W. Armstrong		Ac. 8V. 40A.	200	18	up to 3,000	300		8-10 p.m.	
GSX	Knowle, 1, Leighton Road	Geo. Sharp			200 Var.						
GWX	Clifton, Bristol, 3, Glentworth Road	H. D. Griffith		37 Watts	115						
GWX	Yeovil, 1, King Street	G. W. Mortimer College		¼ in. Coil							
GXA	Streatham, S.E.			200 Watts	320			600			
GXC	Canterbury, 43, Marty's Field Road	S. J. Gibbs		20 Watts	200		300 up				
GXF	Northampton, 6, Cowper Street	W. T. Gibson		40 Watts	100	10	200 up	600			
GXI	Northampton, 194, Kettering Road	F. J. Harris	10 X	40 Watts	200	6	Up 600	20	1 in. Spark Coil 10 Watts	Tues. Wed. & Sat.	
GXL	North Shields, 54, Military Road	James R. Gray		Accum. 4 v. 20 a.	100				1½ in. coil, drct. cpld. helix, plain	Eve. 7-11.30 p.m. on week-days	
GXN	Bolingbroke Villa, 21, Hornsey Rise, N.	R. C. M. Graham		Ac. 8 Volt 50 Watts	200	10	200-1,200 & 200-7,000	10-500		8-9 p.m.	
GXQ	Ealing, 11, Elders Road	H. Grundy / P. G. Mitchell		50 Watts	200	6	200-7,000	500	Directional to South	Any	
GXR	London, 90, Newman Street, Oxford St.	W. B. Griffith		Secondary Cells	100	9	All	Any			London W'less.
GXS	Ilford, 20, Rutland Road	F. C. Grover	Ilford 686	Secondary Cells	150	10	Up to 4,000			6.30-12 p.m.	
GYX	Muswell Hill, N., "Gwynash," 3, Coniston Road	Philip R. Coursey		48 Watts 100 Watts	300						

H

Official Call Letters.	ADDRESS	NAME	Telephone No.	Power	Transmitting Wave Length (Meters)	Sending Range in Miles	Receiving Wave Length (Meters)	Receiving Range Miles	Remarks Transmitting	Usual Times of Working	Club of which a Member if any
HAX	S. Croydon, 80, Avondale Road	C. Harrison	1406	Accum. 10 Watts	260 100	12	100-3,000	1,500	Quenched Spark Gap	Evenings	
HBX	Belfast, 5, Wilmont Terrace, Lisburn Rd.	Albert A. Blackburn, M.I.E.E., M.I.MECH.E.									W'less. Assoc. America
HHX	Hither Green, 95, Minard Road	H. Hillesdey		12 Watts	200	7	Variable	600	Musical note	Evenings	
HLX	Bath	Col. Hippesley		½ Kw.							
HRX	Canterbury, 4, St. Mary's Street	A. V. Hughes			600				8 in. Coil		
HUX	Derby, Rowditch	A. Hulme			200						
HXA	Liverpool, 18, Elm Hall Drive, Mossley Hill	J. A. Henderson		10 Watts	150	5	4,000	1,000			
HXD	West Malling, High Street	E. Hoad		4 Watts	100	1		1,000	Low note	8-10 p.m.	
HXE	Croydon, 1, Northampton Road, Addiscombe	E. Hart		A.C. Mains 40 Watts	220	10	Up to 4,000	800-1,000	A.C. used on 1½ in. Coil		Croydon W'less Soc.
HXF	Kenley, Surrey, Wayside	E. K. Hunter	Purley 106	Accum. 50 Watts	330	12			Loose coupled	8-10.30 p.m.	London W'less.
HXL	Rawditch, Derby, The Orchard	A. B. Hulme			450	8					
HXO	Wilts. Colne, Chilvester Lodge	P. V. Harris	38X	150 Watts	Varies Usually 200	35		800	Coil. Mercury break Rotary gap, loose c'ple	10-12 p.m.	

Official Call Letters.	ADDRESS	NAME	Telephone No.	Power	Transmitting Wave Length (Meters)	Sending Range in Miles	Receiving Wave Length (Meters)	Receiving Range Miles	Remarks Transmitting	Usual Times of Working	Club of which a Member if any
H—*continued*											
HXP	Ruddington, Notts., Manor Park	Lawrence A. Hind	23 Rdgt'n 134a	Accum. 45 Watts	100	5 to 8	Up to 4,000	800		8–10.30 p.m.	
HXV	Oldham, "West Bank," Napier Street	William M. Holden		Accum. 50 Watts	200	10	200 upwards	1,000		8–12 p.m.	
HXX	Norbury, S.W., 11, Norbury Court Road	L. W. Hayes		Alternating Mains 80 Watts	270–300	10–20	About 300	500	Rotary gap to be used, aerial operating room	Any time after 6 p.m.	
HXY	Heckmondwike, Yorks., High Street	P. Hanson		Accum. 8 volts	200	12		500		Morning and Evening	
HXZ	Surrey, Helford, Limpsfield	A. G. Hansford		40 Watts	200	20–40	100–7,000	1,150			
HUX	Ealing, London, S.W.	W. Hodgson		50 Watts	200						
I											
IAX	Catford, S.E., 30, Birkhill Road	A. Irwin		Accum. 20 Watts	200	6	Variable	600	Slightly musical note	Evenings	
IBS	Sheffield, Brincliffe, Lee Crest	J. F. H. Suman			100–200	5		525		6–10p.m.Sun 9a.m.–10p.m.	
ICX	Catford, S.E., 56, Balloch Road	G. C. Farthing		Accum. 20 Watts	200	6	200 up	6			
IJX	Putney, 75, Deodar Road	W. H. Clegg									
IQX	Sowerby Bridge, Throstle Nest	R. Clay								7–10 p.m.	
IXE	Sutton, Surrey, Westward House, Grove Road	L. J. Hancock		50	200	10	Any	400	Loose-coupled	After 6	
IXF	Willesden, London, 387, High St., N.W.	H. Hewett		Mains 10 Wts Secondary Batteries	100	6	200–5,000	800		8–10 p.m.	
IXH	Norwood, 81, South Norwood Hill, S.E.	E. J. Housden			200	10	Up to 3,000	1,000			
IXI	Ilford, Ingram's Commercial and Wireless School	Mrs. C. E. Ingram	142 Ilford.	30 Watts					Used chiefly by Pupils Ingrams W.T.S., Ilford		
IXN	Forest Hill, S.E., Chislon House, Lowther Hill	W. & K. Kolubowicz		Mains & Ac. 20 Watts	100	10	Up to 8,000	1,000		Evenings and Sundays	London W'less
IXS	Everton, Liverpool, 55, Mill Road	W. Holmes		Accum. 10 Watts	100	10	100–7,000	800		7–10 p.m.	Everton W'less
IXX	Kingston-on-Thames, 10a, Fairfield Rd.	— Clifton act		25	200	10		900			
IXV	Wimbledon Park, "High Legh," Leopold Avenue.	N. H. Hamilton									
IVX	Hale, Cheshire, Claremont Grove, "Oakdene"	B. E. Cook		100 Watts	250	10–15		3,500		7–10 p.m.	Radio Scientific
J											
JCX	Welland, Malvern, Brook End	M. Jeynes		$\frac{1}{4}$ Kw.	430						
JDX	Blaina, Mon.., 2, Parrot Row	J. Jones									
JFE	Elland, Lancs., 9, Myrtle Road	G. ford			210	5					
JHX	Mellor, Derbyshire, The Manor House	William Jowett	7a	Accum. 6 volts	100		100	300	Used chiefly by B.P. Scouts	Evenings	
JIX	Mellor, Derbyshire, Drill Hall, B.P. Scouts	William Jowett			150		150	300		Evenings	

Official Call Letters.	NAME	ADDRESS	Telephone No.	Power	Transmitting Wave Length (Meters)	Sending Range in Miles	Receiving Wave Length (Meters)	Receiving Range Miles	Remarks Transmitting	Usual Times of Working	Club of which a Member if any
J—*continued*											
JIX	L. H. Johnson	Colchester, Lion Walk		Accum.	200		100 up	90		8–12 p.m.	
JOX	H. James	Huntly, Aberdeenshire, Devon House		20 Watts	200	20	100 to 7,000	1,000		Evenings	
JRX	L. Johnson	Pitsmoor, Sheffield, Park View, Hinde House Lane					300–500	1,600			
JTX	Rev. G. T. Johnson	Bexhill, Trederwyn, The Down		100 Watts	480	20				6.30–7.30p.m	
JVX	T. H. Hudson	Bradford, Lister Hills, 59, Lerams Terr.		Accum.	200				Loose-cp'ld.		
JXB	Arthur Jones	Bilston, Staffordshire, 41, Green Lanes		50 Watts	300		3,000			7–9.30 p.m.	
JXC	E. Jagger	Bradford, Hilton Road					300				
JXD	W. G. C. Jackson	Forest Hill, S.E., Reigate Lodge, Wood Vale		50	200	10	Any	400	Loose coupled	After 6	
JXQ	A. Hargreaves	Lancashire, 7, Hindle Street, Slacksteads, Bacup		25 Watts	200	8–10	800–1,000	800	Admirality type 2 wire	Mon. Tue. Sat. evenings 7–10 p.m.	
JXS	W. Holmes	Liverpool, 55, Mill Road, Everton		Accum. 10 Watts	100	10	100–7,000				Everton Wireless
JXX	Johnston, A.	Ealing, 4, Warwick Dene	212 Ealing	50	250	10		1,000		Evening	
JZX	F. K. Crowther	West Bromwich, The Beeches		50	200	50	up to 7,000		Rotary Converter		
K											
KAX	J. St. L. Kirwan	Co. Galway, Ireland District Asylum, Ballinasloe,		120 and 200 Watts Batteries	300	20	200–7,000	1,000		Morning and Night	
KJX	L. Greenwell	Woldingham, Marden Park		¼ Kw. set.					Loose Coupled		
KSA	J. G. Wilson	Blackrock, Dublin, Ireland, Rock Road,		Accum.	100	4	80–8,000	600	2-in. Coil, musical note	8.45 p.m. and various	
KST	A. Mountfort	Chelsea, 9, Onslow Studios, 183, King's Road	3651 West'n		10	150	200 up	1,200			
KTX	J. Kershaw	Ramsbottom, Lancs., 95, Chatterton Rd.		25 Watts	200	15				7–10 p.m. Sat.2–10p.m. Sun. 10.30– 6 p.m.	
KUX	J. Kershaw	Ramsbottom, Lancs., Holcombe Hill Sta.		25 Watts	200					Week ends 10, 2, 4, 6, 8, 9.39 p.m.	
KXB	Dr. Knott	Purley, Karnak, Woodcote		250 Watts	300						
KXM	Dr. F. C. Knight	Islington London, N., 43, Claremont Square	1963 Central								
KXC	Dr. F. C. Kempster S. F. Harris	Battersea, London, 59, Bridge Road	Field Station	Accum. 4 volt	85	10	up to 300	30		7.30–9.30p.m	13th B.P. Boy Scouts
KXD	R. G. Gardner	Battersea, London, 59, Bridge Road		20 A.	25	10	up to 200	65		2.30–8 p.m. Sat.	
KXX		South Norwood, London, S.E., 26, Enmore Road	131 Croyd'n	20 Watts	150	4	100	500		8–11 p.m.	
KYX	E. W. Kitchin	Markonia, Egmont Road, Sutton, Surrey		Mains 100 Watts	300	20	10,000	2,000		10.30–10.30	London Wireless

Official Call Letters	NAME	ADDRESS	Telephone No.	Power	Transmitting Wave Length (Meters)	Sending Range in Miles	Receiving Wave Length (Meters)	Receiving Range Miles	Remarks Transmitting	Usual Times of Working	Club of which a Member if any
L											
LAX	Alan Darricote	Bolton, Fairholme, New Hall Lane		10 Watts	100	5	300 up	530	Med. mus. note and low rough note.		B'ham W. Assc.
LBX	H. Littley	West Bromwich, 13, Lodge Road		Motor Altnr. normal ½ Kw.	300–500	Not knwn	50–8,000	1,500 approx.	Rotary Gap, loose coupled	7.30–10.30 p.m.	
LIX	F. A. Lewis	Partick, N.B., 33, Clarendon Street		Accum.	200–250	10				7–9 Sat. 2–5	B'ham W. Assc.
LOX	J. Lowe	Derby, White Street		2 in. spark coil. accum.	200	10	8,000	1,000		Various for experiments	
LSX	H. Littley	West Bromwich, Pheonix Works, Swan Village	179 W.B.	50 Watts	200		50–2,500				
LUX	J. Scott Taggart	Bolton Lieutenants		10 Watts	100	5	300 up	530			
LXA	H. J. Lucas	West Malling, Kent, High Street		50 Watts	300	5			Low Note	7–10.30 p.m. Sun. 5–10.30 p.m. Saturdays	
LXD	J. Lindsay	Brighouse, Yorks., 10, Alma Terrace		50 Watts	300	20	Variable	1,000			Derby Wireless
LXE	J. Lindsay	Portable Station, 5 miles' range from No. 1 Station		20 Watts	300	10	Variable				
LXG	M. H. Thomas	Tytherington, nr. Macclesfield, Beech Hall	91 Mccls. field	House spply,	300	20–30	300–7,000	Usual		8–10 p.m.	
LXK	E. M. Lugard	Chester, 8, Hough Green	391	15 Watts, maximum	200	Not known	500	Not known	4 in. Coil	Evenings	
LXL	H. J. Lucas	West Malling, Kent, High Street		50 Watts	450	15	1,400	1,400		Evenings	
LXR	H. Howard	Brighouse, Ivy House		50 Watts	300	20	Variable		Low Note		
LXX	Rev. E. H. Leale	Bexhill, sussex, St. Stephen's Vicarage		50 Watts Accum.	370					9.30–10 a.m. & Evenings	
LYX	A. T. Lee	Derby, Lonsdal Hill			250	10	5,000	1,000			London Wireless & Derby Wireless
LZX	Rev. F. I. W. Sealy	London, E., 154, East India Dock Road	1010 East	8V. 40A. Ac.	100	5	600	300		Varied	
M											
MAX	A. C. Mayman	Hull, 74, Ella street		10 Watts	100	2	up to 3,000	1,000		10 11 p.m.	
MDF	M. D. F.	Beith, Mainshamilton, Ayrshire	51 Bieth	Accum.	200	80–100	200–4,500	800	8–11.30 p.m. Saturdays	7–10.30 a.m. & 4–11 p.m.	
MKX	E. G. Merrick	Bradford, Listerhills	2439 Bradf'd	250 Watts	600	40	Any	800		All times	
MPX	Geo. Sharp	Knoll, Maiden Bradley		10 Watts	200 Var.						
MS	P. O. Little	Radlett, Herts., Gloucester Villa		10 Watts	80–100	15		1,530	Loose Coupled	8–10 or arrangement	Radlett W.

Official Call Letters.	NAME	ADDRESS	Telephone No.	Power	Transmitting Wave Length (Meters)	Sending Range in Miles	Receiving Wave Length (Meters)	Receiving Range Miles	Remarks Transmitting	Usual Times of Working	Club of which a Member if any
M—*continued*											
MRX	A. H. Medgett	Ramsgate, Rosslyn			200	15	200			7-1 p.m. Sat. 2-10 p.m., Sun. 10.30-6	
MVX	H. E. Mabey	Wimbledon, Surrey, Glenholme, Lake Road			up to 300						
MWX	M. A. Watson	Shepherds Bush, London, 129, Coningham Road	1644 New X		300	20		1,500	4-in. Coil	7-12 p.m.	London Wireless
MXA	L. McMichael	Forest Hill, London, 18, Stondon Park		150 Watts	275	40	Up to 10,000	1,500	6-in. Coil	Evenings	
MXB	H. Merton	London, N., 151, Englefield Road			300						
MXE	E. C. Montgomery-Smith, M.C.R.S.	St. John's Wood, London, N.W., 36 Abbey Road	377 Hampstead	50 Watts	200	10		500		10 p.m.	Wireless Soc., Lon.
MXG	William Winslade	Brixton, S.W., 26, Talma Road		Accum. 6 V. Mains 40 Watts	300	15	Variable Up to 6,000	500	Spark Gap	Various	
MXH	H. Moore	Ealing, 21, Waldegrave Road			400			400			
MXI	H. Moore	Ealing, 21, Waldegrave Road		Mains 40 Watts	400		Up to 6,000	400			
MXK	J. G. Monckton	Maidstone		2.8V. 60 A. Accum.	300	8	Up to 8,000	1,300		Evening	
MXL	C. E. Macket	Leytonstone, Essex, 9, Bulliver Road									
N											
NBX	W. Noble	Wokingham, Barkham Manor	4 Wokingham	1/4 Kw.	500	60	Various			2-5, 8.30-12 p.m.	
NCX	N. C. B. Carrick	Catford, London, 6, Thornsbeach Road		30 Watts	120		4,000	300		Evenings and Week Ends	
NIX	T. J. Northy	High Wycombe, Isca, Peterborough Avenue			200	40		320			
NKX	F. G. Norris	Putney, London, S.W., Bleak House, Riverside			200						
NLX	F. R. Harding Newman	Chippenham, Cambs., Soham	3 Fd'hm	Accum. 100 Watts	200	20	2,810			10-11 a.m. 8.30-10.30 p.m.	
NRX	J. Gillett	Maddox Park, Bookham, Surrey								7-10 p.m. Sat. Sun. Mon.	
NXJ	Charles E. Nipper	Lymington, Highfield Cottage, Hants.	11 L'm'gt'n	Accum.	200	70	600	2000			
NXT	G. R. Marsh	Winchester, Twyford, "Mallard Close," Hants.		Accum. 20 Watts	200	568	Variable				
NSX	J. R. Forshaw	Ormskirk, Lancs., "Westville," St. Helens Road		Accum. 50 Watts	200	20	10,000	1,000	30 words per minute	7.30-11.30 p.m.	
NTX	H. F. Newton	Sydenham, London, S.E., 5, Byne Road		10 Watts	100	10	Variable			6.30-11.30 p.m.	
NUX	H. F. Newton	London, S.E., 1st Sydenham B. P. Boy Scouts		10 Watts	100	10	Variable			Sat. Aft'n.- 9 p.m.	

Official Call Letters.	ADDRESS	NAME	Telephone No.	Power	Transmitting Wave Length (Meters)	Sending Range in Miles	Receiving Wave Length (Meters)	Receiving Range Miles	Remarks Transmitting	Usual Times of Working	Club of which a Member if any
N—*continued*											
NXA	Beeston, Notts., 51, Chilwell Road	W. Norbury		Accum. 60 Watts	300	25–30	100–7,000	700		Evenings after 7 p.m.	
NXC	Snaresbrook, Essex, 78, Mornington Rd.	J. E. Nickless		Accum. 50 Watts	200	10	4,000	3,000	Musical note	8.10 p.m.	
NXK	Scarborough Tramways Depôt, Scalby Rd.	W. E. Nicholl	294 Scarborough	50 Watts	200	10	Up to 10,000	1,000	Portable Sta: Call Letters N.X.L.		
O											
OBX	Bath, Somerset, Newton St., Loe	O. H. Bayldon		¼ Kw.	200	10					
OEX	Sale, Cheshire, Lymehust, Priory Road	D. F. Owen		60 Watts	600	15–18	600	500		7–8 p.m.	
OGH	Athenry, Co. Galway, The Villa, Dunsandle	John Kinneen		3-in. spk Acc 50 Watts							
OGX	Gurteen, Ballinasloe, Ireland, St. Kevrils	Rev. P. O'Laughlin		Accum. 20 Watts	600	50	250–4,000	1,500	High note musical	8–11 p.m.	
OIX	Bristol, 7, Cavendish Rd., Westbury-on-Trym	H. Elie-Lefébure		20 Watts	200–300	15		1,000			
OJX	Birmingham, 19, Whitehead Rd., Aston Manor	G. H. Lloyd					200 up.				B'ham W. Asc.
OKX	Manor Pk., London, 21, Wentworth Rd.	B. B. Long		16 Watts Acc.	150	1	600	200		6–10 p.m.	
ONX	London, 14, Thurlestoe Road	L. E. Owen		10 Watts Coil				1,500		8–10 p.m.	
OSX	Ireland, Ballinaslol. "St. Kevrils," Gurteen	P. O'Laughlin			600	50		1,500		8–11 p.m.	
OUX	New Cross, S.E., 218, New Cross Road	Leslie Oldman	New X 646	Accum. 20 Watts	100	15	4,000	1,000		Evng. & Sat. Afternoon	
OXA	Guildford, Surrey, Littlebourne, Warren Road	P. M. S. Blackett	Guildford 396	Accum. 30 Watts	200	3 or 4			1-in. coil loose cpld. tuner		
OXB	Wylde Green, Warwick, Dilkhoosh, Mayfield Road	W. F. Baxter-Bartram	173 Sutton C'df'ld	Accum. 12 Volt 50 Watts	200	About 8	Various	Various		Evening	B'ham W. Asc.
OXD	Leytonstone, Essex, Fermlea,	P. Bryant			200	50–100	up to 4,000	up to 1,000	1-in. Coil	9–12 p.m.	
OXF	Berks, Whitmore Lodge, Sunninghill	U. F. M. Oliver	Ascot 290	D. C. Dynamo 50 Watts					6-in. coil		
OXJ	Walthamstow, 72, Wellington Road, N.E.	E. L. Ball		Accum. 25 Watts	100	5	100–3,000	250	Coil	5–11 p.m.	
OXO	Hull, 68, Marshall St., Newland Avenue	Charles Dyson		108 Volts.	400	30	300–9,000	600	Musical Note fairly high, drt.-cpld helix	Sun. 10–12	Derby Wireless
OXQ	Burton-on-Trent, Repton School	Repton School		D-c. mains, 200 Watts				1,000	6-in. Spark	Various	
OXT	Bradford, 85, Emm Lane	J. Bever		Accum. 50 Watts	200	25	200–8,000	1,500	Coil	7–10 p.m.	
OXX	Bristol, 13, Claremont Rd., Bishopaton	N. Driver									

P

Official Call Letters	Name	Address	Telephone No.	Power	Transmitting Wave Length (Meters)	Sending Range in Miles	Receiving Wave Length (Meters)	Receiving Range Miles	Remarks Transmitting	Usual Times of Working	Club of which a Member if any
PDX	F. Tolchard	Paignton, S. Devon, Oldway	Paignton 6	½ Kw.	300		Up to 8,000	1,000	Cpld. Cret. Trns. Rotary spk. gap	8–9 p.m.	
PFX	S. Perrier	South Norwood, London, S.E., Silverdale, Cargreen Road		A.C. Mains 150 Watts	200–300 400	40		250			
PGX	P. G. Webb	Bow Common Lane, Invicta Works	3633 East	250 Watts Cells	250	20	800	800	Loose coupled	9 a.m. to 6.30 p.m.	London Wireless
PHI	H. Parr	Halifax, Park Place, Parkinson Lane		Accum. 16 V. 8	150–200	5	400–6,000	1,000		8–11 p.m.	
PXG	E. Arnold Pochin	Buxton, Rosthwaite, Lightwood Rd.		Mains 100 Watts	300		8,000	1,500		Evening	Derby & Mnch'tr Radio Scntfc. S.
PXH	P. J. Parminter	Bournemouth, Milton House, St. Leonard's Road		35 Watts	200		Variable				
PXI	F. A. Pales	Neasden, Mddlesex, 19, Mulgrove Road		Accum. 12 Watts	250	5	250 up	300		9 a.m.–7 p.m.	
PXJ	L. Partridge	Walthamstow, E., 38, Wood End Road		Accum. 8 Volts	200	8	420			7.30–10 p.m.	
PXL	A. W. Phillips	Finchley, 32, Etchingham Park Road			200						
PXN	King William's College	Isle of Man, Castletown	No. 9 Castletn	Dynamos & Accum.	200		Up to 8,000	Any	4 in. Spark Coil	All day	
PXT	J. W. Power	London, S.E., Brockley, 51, St. Asaph Road		40 Watts	200	10	5,500	2,000	Low Note, 1½-in Coil	Evenings and Sun. Aft'ns. 8–10 p.m.	
PXV	James F. Perrin	Dulwich, S.E., 57, Underhill Road		Accum. 20 Watts	100	5	Any				
PXY	J. David Paul, Esq., M.A., F.R.G.S.	Isle of Man, The Crofts		Accum. 15 Watts	200		Up to 8,000	Any	1 in. Spark Coil	Evening	London Wireless
PXZ	Officers' Training Corps	Isle of Man, King William's college		Accum. 15 Watts	200		Up to 2,000	800 miles	⅛ in. Spark Coil	During Field Operations & for Practice	
PZX	H. W. Pope	South Norwood, London, S.E., 24, Queens Road			450	10					

Q

Official Call Letters	Name	Address	Telephone No.	Power	Transmitting Wave Length (Meters)	Sending Range in Miles	Receiving Wave Length (Meters)	Receiving Range Miles	Remarks Transmitting	Usual Times of Working	Club of which a Member if any
QAX	S. G. Pettitt	London, N., Stroud Green, 38, Denton Road		S'cndry Bat. 32 Watts	Up to 600	10	200–2,000	500		7–9 p.m.	
QBX	H. Pettitt	London, E., Stratford, 68, Tavistock Road		S'cndry Bat. 32 Watts	Up to 600	10	200–2,000	500		7–9 p.m.	
QCX	E. A. Payne	Colchester, 2, Honywood Road			190	2	up to 800				
QEX	W. H. Prideaux	Torquay, St. Luke's Road, N., Trevadlock									
QGX	Frank Perry, F.C.S.	Tipton, Staffs., Shrubbery Bloomfield,		Accum. 40 Watts	100	6	100–8,000		Tuning helix 12 in. Coil	Evenings	B'ham W. Assoc
QIX	Derby Wireless Club	Derby, 47, Full Street			150	2	3,000	600		Evening	
QOX	C. Wood	Redhill, The Red House	488	20 Watts	250	5				8.30 p.m.	

Q—continued

Official Call Letters	NAME	ADDRESS	Telephone No.	Power	Transmitting Wave Length (Meters)	Sending Range in Miles	Receiving Wave Length (Meters)	Receiving Range Miles	Remarks Transmitting	Usual Times of Working	Club of which a Member if any
QPX	H. Walton	Bermondsey, 36, Ilderton Road		Accum. 50 Watts	200	12	Up to 6,000	1,500	Ignition Coil	Evenings	
QQX	F. G. Perkins	Doncaster, 13, Royal Avenue	119 Doncaster	50 Watts	200						
QRX	R. J. Wittingham	Doncaster, Cusworth			200						
QXJ	Harold Cliffe	Mexborough, nr. Rotherham, 6, Makin Street		Accum. 50 Watts	200		190	500		Evenings	
QXK	George Chalmers	Beeston, Notts, 1, Devonshire Avenue	68 B'stn	Sec. Cells Coil, 100 W.	200	50	6,000		Rotary Spark Gap	9 p.m.–1 a.m.	
R											
RDX	E. Ryves	Leamington Spa, Ranston, Northumberland Road		1/4 Kw.	240	20	250–5,000	400		9–10.30 p.m.	
REX	W. Ryley	Croydon, London, Hazlemere, Chichester Road		40 Watts	200	10	4,000	400		7–10 p.m. Sat.3–10 p.m.	
RJX	D. H. Rose	Heaton, Newcastle-on-Tyne, 5, Simonside Terr.			200				1-in. Coil		
RKX	R. H. Klein	W. Hampstead, London, 18, Crediton Rd.	2959 Hampstead	40 Watts	250	50	300	600–1,000	8-in. Coil	8.30 p.m. and Sun. mornings	L. W., Derby W.
RLX	R. Lowe	Warrington, 159, Winwick Road		20 Watts	100–150	30	100 up				
ROX	O. H. Relly	Eastbourne, De Roos Road		124 Watts	100	10–15	100 up				
RPX	R. de la Rue	Newmarket, Six Mile Bottom		80 Watts	200	10–15					
RQX	R. de la Rue	Cambridge, Hobson Street		80 Watts	200	8					
RRX	C. W. Raffety	East Croydon, 12, Altyre Road		Accum. 18 Watts	About 180–250			1,000	Rotary gap	After 8 p.m.	
RVX	W. H. Rhodes	Bradford, 42, Derby Street, Gt. Horton		30 Watts	200						
RVX	A. J. Redman	Forest Gate, London, 100 Windsor Rd.		10 Watts	150						
RWX	R. West	Honor Oak Park, London, 109, Stondon Park		50 Watts	150				Musical note	10 a.m. and evenings	
RXA	T. P. Rushton	Newport, Bucks, 4, Abbey Terrace									
RXD	R. H. N. Dawson	London, N., 48, Clevedon Mansions, Highgate Road		50 Watts	00						
RXE	R. H. Rogers	Birmingham, 229, Balsall Heath Road		Acc. 50 Wts.	200	10	up to 8,000	1,000			B'ham W. Asc
RXK	W. J. & W. R. Kingston	Brighton, 11, Davidgon Road		Acc. 100 Wts.	200	20	4,000	800		Evenings after 6 p.m.	
RXN	A. N. Roberts, B.Sc.	Wakefield, Grange Moor		50 Watts	300	25		Long D'stnce Stat'ns			London Wireless
RXY	Barrow and District Amateur W. Assoc., Sec., E. Redpath, 19, NIger Street, Vickerstown	Barrow-in-Furness, Market Street			200						
RYX	R. H. Reece	Kent, Birchington Basketts		Acc. 10 Wts.	100	5	100 up	2,500		Jan. Aug. Sept. Dec.	London Wireless

Official Call Letters	NAME	ADDRESS	Telephone No.	Power	Transmitting Wave Length (Meters)	Sending Range in Miles	Receiving Wave Length (Meters)	Receiving Range Miles	Remarks Transmitting	Usual Times of Working	Club of which a Member if any
R—*continued*											
RZX	R. H. Reece	Kent, Birchington Basketts		Acc. 10 Wts.	100	1	100	300	Portable set l'cn's'd to work within 1 mile of Basketts.	Jan. Aug. Sept. Dec.	
S											
SAX	P. L. Stokoe	Blyth, 5, Princess Gardens		Accum. 20 Watts	100	5	Up to 100	5		6–10 p.m.	
SAX	G. Smith	Coventry, 67, Albany Road		60 Watts	80–100	26		25		All day	President Coventry Wireless
SIX	H. Stapleton	Clapham Rise, S.W., 3, Brideaux Rise		Accum. 12 Watts	300	200	250–4,000	600	Slightly musl. note	Evenings	
SJG	S. J. Groves	Thornton Heath, Surrey, 4, Norfolk Rd.		1-in. Coil	150		150–2,000	1,000	Low Note	7.10 p.m.	
SJX	N. F. Scarborough	Halifax, Royd Terrace					200–2,500	2,000		Evenings	
SMF	W. Harewod Moon	Sully, Nr. Cardiff, "Mayfield"					160 up	4,500			
SMX	A. Stapley	Tunbridge Wells, 57, Calverden Pk. Rd.			250						
SOX	R. Spencer	Blackburn, Holytree House, Cherrytree	294		300–100		600–3,000	800	4 in. S'pk Coil	10–12 a.m.	
SRI	H. Buckley	Co. Down. Holywood, Marino, Clanbrassil	3337 Dublin							8–11 p.m.	
SUN	C. Ross	Larne, Ireland, Sun Laundry	23Larne	50 Watts		5–10	300–7,000	500		9.30 p.m.	
SXB	N. H. Swinstead	Highgate, London, N., 15, Avenue Rd.		Accum-		1				8–9.30 p.m.	
SXC	P. L. Shaw	Harrow-on-the-Hill, Middlesex, Maxted Park, "The Staithe."			300		300 and up	500	Ignition Coil		
SXD	E. Sykes	Stockton-on-Tees, "Fingarth," Richmond Road	364 Stcktn	Accum. 50 Watts	200	10	Any	400		6–10 p.m.	
SXF	W. G. Stockall	Stroud Green, London, N., 50, Ferme Park Road		20 Watts	300	5	5,000	1,000		7–11 p.m.	
SXI	H. B. Sayer	Oxton, Birkenhead, The Vicarage,	1194 Birkenhead	Accum. 10 Watts	100	4	100–1,000	750	Closed circuit	8–10.15 p.m.	
SXM	A. Spedding, Junr.	Dewsbury, "Oakley Villas," Oxford Rd.		Batteries 100 Watts	300						
SXN	F. C. Spurr	Birmingham, 62, Wheelwright Road, Erdington		30 Watts	200						
SXS	H. L. Stringer	Kenilworth, Warwick, Park Hill	9 Kenilworth	Accum. 40 Watts	150–200	5	200–1,000	1,000		10.15 a.m. & 10.15 p.m.	
T											
TAX	S. G. Taylor	Derby, St. Mary's Gate		10 Watts	250	5	8,000	1,000	Loose coupled	8–10.30 p.m.	
TBX	J. T. Burrell	Boreham Wood, Herts, Clovendon Road	99 Radlett		80–100	15		1,500			Radlett W.
TBX	G. W. Tonkin	Bristol, 20, Northumberland Road, Redland		Accumulator 20 Watts	200	5	150	600	Low note, speed 15 words p. m.	7–8 a.m. 9–10 p.m.	Bristol W. Assoc.
TEX	H. F. E. Trigg	Bournemouth, "Cliff House," East Cliff	1637	Accum. 60 Watts	600	25	300	300	Ordinary cp'ld.	8–10 p.m.	

Official Call Letters	ADDRESS	NAME	Telephone No.	Power	Transmitting Wave Length (Meters)	Sending Range in Miles	Receiving Wave Length (Meters)	Receiving Range Miles	Remarks Transmitting	Usual Times of Working	Club of which a Member if any
T—continued											
TFX	Bristol, 66, Stapleton Road	G. W. Tonkin	2479X4 Bristol	Under Construction			100	300		5.30 p.m. for few minutes	
TGX	Bexhill, Gilling	H. Tomlinson		60 Watts	480					6–7.30 p.m.	
TOX	S.W., Streatham, London, 79, Stanthorpe Road	D. W. Thompson		10 Watts	300	2					
TSK	Kensington, London, 74, Cathcart Studio, Redcliffe Road	T. S. K.		Accum.					1/2-in. Coil		
TSX	Banbury, Middleton Cheney	H. G. Treadwell		6 in. Coil	500	50 or more				Day and night	
TTX	Teddington, 22, Manor Road	G. Tough	173 Rich'd	40 Watts Accum.	210		4,000	1,000			
TWX	Twickenham, London Road, "Hurstcroft"	W. J. Shaw		200 Watts	420	420	30		6 in. Coil		
TXG	Liverpool, 57, Sandown Lane, Wavetree	Leonard Turton		Sec. Batt. 4 Volts	100		Up to 8,000	1,000			
TKK	Kendal, Beech Bank	W. K. Alford		25 Watts	200	5					
TXR	52, The Avenue, Muswell Hill	A. E. Tyler		2ndy Batts 30 Watts	200	10	Up to 3,000	1,000	Used by Students		
TXS	Birmingham, Geoffrey Buildings, John Bright Street	Birmingham Wireless Association		Accum.	200		200–4,000			After 7.30	B'ham W. Assc. Secy.
TXX	Liverpool, 33 Prince Alfred Rd., Wavertree	J. A. Critchley		50 Watts	100	15		400			
TCX	Derby, Wilkinson Memorial School										
TYX	London, W.., 8, Craven Hill	W. Tingey		10 Watts	250	5	500				
TZX	Birmingham, Brentwood, Solihull	J. B. Tucker	51 Solih'll	Accum. 50 Watts	200	15	200 to 8,000	1,000	2-in. Coil		
U											
UAX	Bowden, Cheshire, The Elms, Vale Road	A. L. Megson		Accum. 10 Watts	200	20	Up to 10,000	2,000		Evenings	Cheshire Radio S. Soc.
UBX	Bowden, Sundal, Portland Road	G. G. Boullen			200		250 up	250			
UDX	Esperanza Cottage, Suffolk Stoke-by-Wayland.	L. W. C. Martin		Accum. 30 Watts	450 & 300	20	Up to 4,600	700–1,000	Inductive coupling		
UEX	Ditto Radius of 10 miles	L. W. C. Martin		Accum. 30 Watts	450 & 300	10	Up to 2,800	500	Auto Jigger		
UOX	4, Waterpath Square, Chester	T. J. Matthews		50 Wts. Acm.	200	20				Saturday and Sunday	
UPX	Wimbledon, London, Merton Hall Road	H. Wynn Moser		50	300	3	4,000	300		Uncertain	L'pool W. Asso.
URX	Derby, Junction Street	G. E. Mart			200			600			
USX	Bexhill, 1, Collington Avenue	J. E. Maynard	378 Bexhill	50 Watts	150	25–30		1,000		Evenings	
UVX	Wimbledon, London, Glenholme Lake Road			Accum. 50 Watts	300	12	Up to 10,000	1,000		8–11 p.m.	
UXD	Newport, 30, Milman Street			10 Watts	100				1/2-in. Coil		
UXG	East Dulwich, 125, Goodrich Road,	V. Stagg		60 Watts	300	10				Evenings	

Official Call Letters	NAME	ADDRESS	Telephone No.	Power	Transmitting Wave Length (Meters)	Sending Range in Miles	Receiving Wave Length (Meters)	Receiving Range Miles	Remarks Transmitting	Usual Times of Working	Club of which a Member if any
U—*continued*											
UXQ	G. Sutton	Dulwich, S.E., 18 Melford Road.		Accum. 50 Watts	200				Mlt. Spk. Gap, Cry. & Sil. D.	7–10 p.m.	
UKU	W. C. Smith	Lancashire, 9, Hindle Street, Slacksteads, Bacup		40 Watts	200	10–15		800–1,000	Aerial Admrlty type 2-Wire	Mon., Thurs., Sat. evenings	
V											
VAX	Vivian B. Learoyd	Huddersfield, Elm Bank	808 H'ddersfield	¼ K W	600	40	100–7,000		Rotary Gap	9 p.m. Sunday 5–9 p.m.	
VCX	G. D. L. Harcourt	Bushey Heath, 55, Merry Hill Mount		20 Watts	100		Variable	600		Various	
VGX	A. Burrows	Lewisham, London, S.E., 30, Courthill Road		12 Watts	200	7					
VJX	R. Hodges	Carlton, Notts., Crail Villa, Gedling Road		50 Watts	250	8	200–7,000	600			
VLX	F. Horace Hulme	Birkenhead, 23, Cavendish Drive, Rock Ferry		Accum. Max. Output 30 Watts	200	20	200–7,000	600	Heard interruptions from other Station while Transmitting	8–10.30 p.m. and odd times	
VSX	N. B. D. Hyde	Seacombe, Cheshire, 19, Percy Road		10 Watts	100		Variable			Fri. & Sat. Ev'gs 12 p.m.	
VXA	Magnus Volk	Selborne, Hassocks	51 Hassocks	Transformer &c.	250 Metres	40	UP to 6,000	1,000			London Wireless
VXD	C. W. Valtings	Bickley, Kent, "Heath Bank"	1203 Bromley		200	2	200–1,800	1,250		5–10 p.m.	
VXN	Arthur W. Bridges	Newcastle-on-Tyne, 53, Greystone Ave.		Accum. 24 Watts	150		150	700	Loose Coupled		N'wc'le & D.W.A.
VXO	W. L. Mountford	Loughton, Essex, "Glenowen," High Beech Road		16 Watts	150						
VXR	E. A. Barker	Barnsley, Electricity Works		250 Watts Accum.	300		300				
VXT	W. A. Vaughan	Lancs., Bolton, 57, Shrewsbury Road		25 Watts Accum.	300		200–8,000	2,000	10 & 5-in. Spk. Coils R. S. Gap 5-in. Spk. Coil.	Evenings, Sat. afternoon.	
VXU	W. A. Vaughan	Bolton, Grecian Cotton Mills, Lever St.		25 Watts	300						
W											
WBX	H. S. Walker	Brentford, Park Lodge									
WCX											
WPX	H. R. Wilkinson	Stoke-by-Nayland, Colchester		¼ Kw.	400–500						
WQX											
WFX	W. H. Foster	Liverpool, 94, Belgrave Road, St. Michaels		10 Watts	100		100 up				
WGX	W. W. Blakeman	Brockley, S.E., 237, Lewisham High Road		10 Watts	200		100–5,000	600		8–10 p.m.	
WKX	M. W. Hobson	Birmingham, Bownes, Grove Avenue, Moseley		Accum. 20 Watts	100	6	100 and above		1-in. Spark Coil		B'ham W. Asc.
WOX	J. A. Walshaw	Leeds, Garnett Villa, Otley	97 Otley	250 and 1 Kw.	Approx. 600	40	150 and above	Malta etc.	Musical	9 p.m.	

Official Call Letters.	ADDRESS	NAME	Telephone No.	Power	Transmitting Wave Length (Meters)	Sending Range in Miles	Receiving Wave Length (Meters)	Receiving Range Miles	Remarks Transmitting	Usual Times of Working	Club of which a Member if any
W—*continued*											
WUX	Warminster, 21, George St.	I. Claude Willcox		¼ Kw.	600				Musical note		B'ham W. Asc.
WVX	Birmingham, Oakland, Fox Hollies Rd., Acocks Green	W. D. Vick		Accum. 10 Watts	100	6	100 to 2,000		½-in. Coil and Helix.		
WXA	Sutton, "St. Olaves," Mulgrave Road	R. I. Wells		Mains 50 W.	200						
WXD	Leytonstone, London, 87, Matcham Road	G. Whitton			200		up to 8,000	1 200		8.30 p.m.	
WXF	Clitheroe, Lancs., 80, Chalburn Road										
WXH	Epsom, Aroona, College Road	Capt. H. Lee Wright, R.E.	467 Epsom	120	350–400	15	100–4,000	800		8.30 p.m. and Sundays, also any time by appointment.	
WXX	"Eversley" Godstone Road, Purley	F. R. Weatherstone		Batts 120 W.	300–600	15	600	1,000		Evenings	Purley Radio
Y											
YAX	Birr, King's Co., Ireland, Cumberland St.	C. W. Browne		¼ Kw.	300	40	3,500	800–1,000	4-in. Coil, L'dn. Jar Condensers, Auto-Jigger	9–11 p.m.	
YDX	Blackpyl, nr. Swansea, "Oakleigh"	Arthur Percy Brown	14Y Skelty Sw'ns'a	Accum. 84 Watts	450	15					
YEX	Blackpool, Claremont Park, Upperhill,	E. F. Biddiscombe		Accum. 50 Watts	200	15–20	up to 7,000	500–600		Any time	
YFX	Poulton le Fylde, Oaklea	G. H. Buckley	29	Accum. 50 Watts	600	8	200–7,000	800		Holidays and Week Ends	
YHX	Forest Gate, London, E., 104, Clova Rd.	E. W. Braendle	7590 Central	12 Watts	250	1	600	100	High note	6.10 p.m.	
YIX	3, Bull Street, Birmingham	H. Beresford		Accum.	300	10	500	700		Evening	B'ham W. Assc.
YJX	St Heliers, Highbridge Road, Wylde Green	H. Beresford		Accum.	300	10	700	1,000		Evening	B'ham W. Assc.
YMX	Peckham Rye, London, 16, Carden Road	W. L. Barrett		Accum. 40 Watts	30–600	10	varies	1,000		7–10 p.m.	
YPX	Keithley, Yorks., Thwaites Brow	B. Blenkiron		100 Watts	600	30	various	1,000	Rotary Gap Motor Ignition Coil	8.30–11 p.m. 9–10 a.m.	
YUX	Streatham, London, S.W., Homewood, 73, Babington Road	R. H. Barthel		Accum. 12 Watts	350	4	up to 7,000			3.30–10 p.m.	
YXS	Wetherby, Yorkshire, "The Mount"	H. B. Lee			200			500		7 p.m.–midn't	
Z											
ZBX	Wednesfield, Helmsley Lodge	J. V. Waine (Portable)		110 V. Motor Gen.	100–300	100	100–6,000	1,000		All Day	
ZCX	Harrogate, "The Priory," "Trinity Road"; Kensington, 40, Queen's Gate; Stourbridge, "Ivy Cottage," Olant St.	V. P. Webb			600		Various	2,000			
ZFX	Newick, Sussex, Patterdale	R. M. West		Accum. 10 Watts	600						
ZKX	Westcliffe, Godolphin, Park Road	T. B. Wiltshire			217						

Z—continued

Official Call Letters.	NAME	ADDRESS	Telephone No.	Power	Transmitting Wave Length (Meters)	Sending Range in Miles	Receiving Wave Length (Meters)	Receiving Range Miles	Remarks Transmitting	Usual Times of Working	Club of which a Member if any
ZNX	D. Sinclair	Nunhead, London, 8, Homeleigh Road, Waverley Park		20 Watts Accum.	180		180–5,000		1-in. Coil	Evenings	
ZTX	H. R. Wooden	Finsbury Park, London, N., 329, Green Lanes		50 Watts Accum.	200		100–7,000	200		6–8 p.m.	
ZUX	T. D. Wright	Birmingham, Olton, Ulverley Road		8 Watts Accum.	200	4	200 and above		½-in. Coil and Helix.		
ZXG	T. Boutland, Junr.	Northumberland, 25 First Row Ashington		50 Watts Accum.	200	7	5,000	500		12–1 p.m. 6–8 p.m.	
ZXH	T. Boutland, Junr.	Northumberland, 25 First Row Ashington		50 Watts Accum.	200	7	500	100		Sundays only	
ZXB	E. Redpath	Barrow-in-Furness, 19 Niger Street, Vickerstown		50 Watts	200	25	8,000	Long Dis. Sta.		10–1 p.m. 8–11 p.m.	Barrow A.W.A.
ZXK	George Daniel Plomer	Eastbourne, Sussex, 107, Enys Road	6 Cottishall	2-in. Coil 30 Watts	200	5–10				On and off	
ZXU	Michael Birkbeck	Norwich, Stratton, Strawless Hall		100v'lt Circ't 60 Watts	250	25	250 upwards	1,500		10–12 p.m.	Cavendish Cl'b

Index